The Random Book of...

PAUL

Well, I didn't know that!

All statistics, facts and figures are correct as of March 31st 2009.

Published By:

Stripe Publishing Ltd
First Floor, 3 St. Georges Place, Brighton, BN1 4GA

Email: info@stripepublishing.co.uk
Web: www.stripepublishing.co.uk

First published 2009

10-digit ISBN: 1-907158-07-3
13-digit ISBN: 978-1-907158-07-0

Printed and bound by Gutenberg Press Ltd., Malta.

Editor: Dan Tester
Illustrations: Jonathan Pugh (www.pughcartoons.co.uk)
Typesetting: Andrew Searle
Cover: Andy Heath

To Alison, my light

Paul Reaney – March 2009

INTRODUCTION

It's a strange thing being called Paul.

I mean, it's the sort of name that does exactly the opposite to what it says on the tin – it doesn't mark you out, it sort of makes you anonymous.

Pauls are not Theodores or Winstons or Sebastians, they're Pauls – benign, banal and boring. Or so you might think.

The Pauls contained herein prove beyond all reasonable and rational doubt that rather than being anonymous, Pauls are indeed omnipotent.

We are kings and rulers, thieves and vagabonds, killers and pillars, men of pen and sword, thinkers, tinkers, soldiers, spies.

It's not that the world doesn't sit up and take notice of Pauls; we are proud men who don't like to shout about our achievements, we quietly go along our merry way just simply writing Eleanor Rigby, founding Cubism or rescuing Rwanda from the edge of civil collapse.

That's what we do, us Pauls – everything.

We are men of integrity, decency and honour who also happen to have founded *Razzle*, killed around 3,500 people while a Colombian drug baron and helped create The Jonas Brothers.

So go forth, be proud and wear your name proudly. You are a Paul.

Paul Reaney – March 2009

PAUL – THE BACKGROUND

Paul, a common English name, was originally derived from Paulus, a nomen (the second of three usual names) or cognomen (third of three names) of ancient Rome. The name is of Latin origin meaning 'humble'.

The name **Paul** could be dwindling in British popularity. According to the Office for National Statistics, Paul was the UK's seventh most popular name in 1954. In 1964 it had become the second most popular name and in 1974 there were more men named Paul than any other! In 1984, the nation was growing tired of Paul as it slumped to ninth and in 1994 it was no longer in the top ten. Surely there's been some mistake?

The name Paul has spawned surnames across Europe, being as surnames are often patronymic (a personal name based on the name of one's father). For example Pol, Pawel, Paal, Powley, Polini, Pavelka, Paulson, Polvsen, Bogosian and Pavkin are all based on a father called Paul.

Looking for a derivative slant on the name Paul? Ask our non-English speaking brothers to throw one up...

Albanian:	**Pali**
Armenian:	**Poghos** (in Eastern Armenian) or **Boghosm**
Arabic:	**Bulus**
Belarusian:	**Paval**
Bosnian:	**Pavle**

Bulgarian:	**Pavel**
Catalan:	**Pau**
Croatian:	**Pavel**
Czech:	**Pavel**
Danish:	**Poul, Povl**
Dutch:	**Paulus**
Faroese:	**Páll**
Finnish:	**Paavali, Paavo Pauli**
Greek:	**Pávlos**
Hebrew:	**Shaul**
Hungarian:	**Pál**
Icelandic:	**Páll**
Irish:	**Pól**
Italian:	**Paolo**
Japanese:	**Pōru**
Korean:	**Pol**
Latin:	**Paulus**
Latvian:	**Pauls, Pāvils**
Lithuanian:	**Paulius, Povilas**
Malayalam:	**Paulose**
Macedonian:	**Pavle**
Maltese:	**Pawl, Pawlu**
Norwegian:	**Pål**
Polish:	**Paweł**
Portuguese:	**Paulo**
Roman:	**Pavle**
Romanian:	**Pavel**
Russian:	**Павел (Pável)**
Scottish Gaelic:	**Pòl**
Serbian:	**Pavle or Pol**
Slovak:	**Pavol**
Slovene:	**Pavel**

Spanish:	**Pablo**
Swedish:	**Pål**
Ukrainian:	**Pávlo**

PAULS YOU COULD ASK ROUND FOR TEA...

Nottingham-based designer **Sir Paul Smith**, knighted in 2001, has described his designs as Savile Row meets Mr. Bean. He always wanted to be a professional cyclist until an accident scuppered his plans and set him on a new course. It proved lucrative – his business is worth an estimated £300 million per year.

The 55-year-old **Paul Allen** founded Microsoft, initially Micro-Soft, with Bill Gates in 1975. According to the US Forbes Rich List, he's now worth around $22.5b. Allen left Microsoft in 1983 after a battle with Hodgkin's disease but remains a member of the board. He is also the main investor/founder of Ticketmaster, as well as owner of basketball team the Portland Trailblazers and American football team Seattle Seahawks. Allen bankrolled the Experience Music Project, inspired by Jimi Hendrix, and SpaceShipOne, the first private flight into suborbital space. Paul Allen's total lifetime giving is estimated to be around $900 million.

Paul Tudor Jones II, the famous US commodity trader worth $2.5 billion, is ranked the 369th richest person in the world.

Pauls you would not ask round for tea...

Paul Bernardo and wife Karla Homolka were known as the Canadian Ken and Barbie of serial killers and operated in the mid to late 1980s. Having already raped nine girls, the first unfortunate murder victim was Homolka's 15-year-old sister Tammy who they drugged and raped. She eventually choked on her own vomit. The second was 14-year-old Leslie Mahaffy, who was kidnapped, raped and beaten for over 24 hours before being strangled with an electrical cord, dismembered, and encased in blocks of cement.

On the day Mahaffy was discovered (because the cement had broken apart under the water), Bernardo and Homolka got married. The 15-year-old Kirsten French was their third victim. She was kidnapped – after Homolka posed as a lost tourist – and dragged into the pair's car. Homolka testified that Bernardo strangled French for exactly seven minutes while she watched.

Compared to **Paul John Knowles**, Bernardo was a part-timer. Knowles, aka the Casanova killer, was, in 1974, linked to the deaths of 18 people though he claimed the number should have been nearer 35. At trial, the good looking and unrepentant murderer described himself as "the most successful member of my family". Knowles met a suitable death. While riding in the back of a police car on his way to find a murder weapon used to kill a highway patrolman and business man, he used a hidden paperclip to unlock his handcuffs.

Knowles grabbed the driving sheriff's handgun and fired. The detective in the car drew his gun and shot Knowles dead in the back seat. Some claim the killing was revenge for Knowles' murder of a fellow state trooper. At his funeral, it is reported that the minister refused to pray that his soul would rest in peace.

The family of **Paul Devoe III**, the Texas spree killer who was accused of killing six people in August 2007, claim it was rattlesnake-bite medicine that turned him into a killer. Before that, Devoe was a career criminal.

Paul Denyer, aka the Frankston Serial Killer, murdered three women in 1993 in the Melbourne suburb of Frankston. His childhood was littered with signs: his mother recalled him rolling from a table and hurting his head; his brother woke to find Paul banging his head on the front of the bed; he hung the family's kitten from a tree and stole neighbours' underwear off the line and then masturbated with them. A self-confessed misogynist, Denyer has filed for gender-reassignment in a bid to become a woman.

In November 2007, Brit **Paul Durant** was convicted for murdering and dissecting the body of Karen Durrel. Upon his conviction, Durant wrote: "I believed God had delivered her to me and I was getting messages from the telly. After I killed her, I cut her body into small parts, eating what parts of her I found eatable. I finally disposed of what was left in small rubbish bags." He said his remaining mission in life was to "kill and eat paedophiles".

President of Cameroon since 1982, **Paul Biya** is featured in historian David Wallechinsky's *Tyrants, the World's 20 Worst Living Dictators*. On his electoral process, Wallechinsky comments: "Every few years, Biya stages an election to justify his continuing reign, but these elections have no credibility. In fact, Biya is credited with a creative innovation in the world of phoney elections. In 2004, annoyed by the criticisms of international vote-monitoring groups, he paid for his own set of international observers, six ex-U.S. congressmen, who certified his election as free and fair." In 2007, *Parade* magazine ranked Biya the 19th worst dictator in the world.

Pablo Escobar – aka El Patrón or El Doctor – the Colombian drug lord was listed, in 1989, as the seventh richest man in the world. Absolutely ruthless in his pursuit of power, he is reportedly responsible for killing 30 judges, 457 policemen and a further 3,500 people. It is also reported that Escobar began his criminal career while he was still in school by stealing tombstones and selling them to Panama smugglers. Escobar created and lived in the luxurious Naples Ranch estate. After his death, the estate, ranch and zoo were given to low-income families under the domain extinction law. It is being converted into a theme park.

Son of a Sicilian immigrant, gangster **Paul Castellano** was eventually gunned down in broad daylight by John Gotti's men outside Sparks Steak House in Manhattan. Castellano joined 'The Business' as a kid running errands for mob-controlled bookies. At 19 he was caught in an armed robbery but didn't squeal on his accomplices, thus earning respect. He was a negotiator, not a killer, and while alive organised a truce with the leaders of the Irish New York Mafia. His house was bugged by the FBI and recordings linked him to 24 murders. Set for jail, and possible plea-bargain, Gotti struck.

Where did it all go wrong? Australian **Paul Hayward** had played professional rugby league with the Newtown Jets and been selected to represent Australia at the 1976 Montreal Olympics in boxing. Then, shortly before the games, he was convicted in Thailand for attempting to export 8.5 kg of heroin back into Australia. He received a 30-year sentence, but was released on April 7th 1989, after being granted a royal pardon. To make matters worse, in jail Hayward became a heroin user and contracted HIV and tuberculosis. He died of a heroin overdose in 1992.

There's no place like death row for **Paul John Fitzpatrick**. The accused murderer was re-convicted after a new trial. However, after a spell with normal prisoners, he put in a request to return to death row claiming: "It's just a hell of a lot easier doing time with murderers than it is with fools... I probably found the most peace I've ever had in my whole life on death row. It's the calmest place I've ever been."

PAPAL PAULS

There have been six Popes named Paul.

Pope Paul I (757-67)	was the 94th
Paul II (1464-71)	212th
Paul III (1534-1549)	221st
Paul IV (1555-59)	224th
Paul V (1605-21)	234th
Paul VI (1963-78)	263rd

The first Pope was St. Peter (between 32-67AD) and most recent Benedict XVI, the 265th, who began his reign in 2005.

Pope Paul I introduced the umbrella to Germany. Paul bestowed upon King Pepin the Short a jewel-handled umbrella as a token of Papal support for Pepin's Frankish reign.

After **Pope Paul II**'s death, one of his successors suggested that he should be called Maria Pietissima, 'Our Lady of Pity', because he was inclined to break into tears at times of crisis. However, other commentators have suggested that the nickname was due to PP II's propensity to enjoy dressing up in the finest ecclesiastical finery, a trend that spawned whispers of homosexuality.

Bearded **Pope Paul III** lies buried in St. Peter's Michelangelo-designed tomb. Paul oversaw the complete restoration of Catholic faith and piety. He was the man who, in 1545, championed and eventually opened The Council of Trent. It ran for just 18 years until 1563 but executed a thorough reform of the inner life of the Church including defining Protestant heresies and Church teachings of Scripture and Tradition, Original Sin, Justification, Sacraments, the Eucharist in Holy Mass and the veneration of saints. Paul was also one of the few Popes to have fathered children before his election.

At 78, **Pope Paul IV** was the third oldest Pope at the time of taking office. The Vicar of Christ upon Earth between 1476 and 1559, he was a rigid, severe, unbending man, a purist and true Italian nationalist who firmly believed: "Extra Ecclesiam nulla salus" (outside the Church there is no salvation). He created the Roman Ghetto for Jews where they were locked in at night and made to wear yellow hats (men) and veils or shawls (women). Paul also introduced the *Index Librorum Prohibitorum (Index of Prohibited Books)* to Venice in order to ban all books written by Protestants, as well as Italian and German translations of the Latin Bible.

Pope Paul V was equally stern and unyielding. A lawyer rather than diplomat, who fiercely defended the privileges of the Church, he was Pope at a time of two major challenges; to science and the state. In 1616, he warned Galileo not to defend or uphold the heliocentric ideas of Copernicus; the Church wanted the Earth, not the Sun, to remain the centre of their universe. He then oversaw Venice pass two new laws which, for the first time, saw the state and church separated.

Paul's response was to place an injunction on Venice. This meant a suspension of all public worship in the city.

"A dimple on the chin, the devil within" **Pope Paul VI**

Pope Paul VI – born Giovanni Battista Enrico Antonio Maria Montini – took on the name Paul to indicate a renewed global mission to spread the message of Christ. Rumour surrounded him. It was claimed that an actor substituted for him in certain public appearances, beginning in 1975. The claim was made by followers of Our Lady of Fatima. This was the title given to the Blessed Virgin Mary by those who believe that she appeared to three shepherd children at Fátima, Portugal on the thirteenth day of six consecutive months in 1917. **Paul** was the last Pope to be crowned with the Papal Tiara. His decision to abandon its use was highly controversial with traditionalists. Many Catholics continue to campaign for its re-introduction.

The Conversion of **Saint Paul** is celebrated on January 25th and recounts the *Conversion of Saul of Tarsus to Christianity* when he would become the Apostle **Paul**. While on the road to Damascus (36AD) to annihilate the Christian community, Saul of Tarsus was blinded by a brilliant light and heard Christ's voice saying, "Saul, Saul, why persecutest thou me?" Saul of Tarsus would journey into Damascus, where he was cured, being baptised into Christianity. The Christian theological implication of the Conversion of Paul is that it witnesses the absolution of sin that is offered by faith and grace through belief in Christ.

UNDERWATER PAULS

St. Paul's Fingerfin, or *Nemadactylus monodactylus*, is a species of morwong fish native to the waters around Île Saint-Paul and Île Amsterdam in the Indian Ocean. The fish reaches a size of approximately 60cm and feeds on both bottom-dwelling and open-water organisms.

⟫⟪⟫

VISIT PAUL!

Paul is a village and civil parish in the Penwith district of Cornwall. The majority of Paul falls in the Penzance South ward and the village's parish church is said to have been founded in 490 by Welsh Saint Paul Aurelian. Paul is resolute, being one of the communities destroyed in the Spanish raid of 1595 carried out by Carlos de Amésquita (one of only two times that Spanish soldiers have disembarked in England). The (disputed) last native speaker of Cornish, Dolly Pentreath, lies in Paul beneath a memorial placed there by Louis Lucien Bonaparte, nephew of Napoleon, in the 19th century. The feast of Paul is held on the Sunday nearest to 10th October every year when the village is decorated and a civic service takes place. A week prior, the village worships a former local bus driver of the same name!

The city of **Paul** in Minidoka County, Idaho, USA contains, according to the 2000 US census, a population of 998 people and 276 families. The average income of those households, in 1999, was $30,417 – over $10,000 below the national level. The average household size is 2.44 and the average family size 2.99. The lucky kids go to Paul Elementary School. The first records of the town date back to 1907 when settlers came to work on the construction of the Minidoka Dam and, a little later, the railroad. Today, agriculture dominates Paul's way of life thanks to the region's rich farmland. Paul lies within the wonderfully named Magic Valley in the Snake River Plain.

St. Paul is the capital city of Minnesota, USA. The earliest known inhabitants, from about 400AD, were members of the Native American Hopewell tradition who buried their dead in mounds – now Indian Mounds Park. The original name of the settlement that became St. Paul was born out of the name of French-Canadian whiskey trader, Pierre 'Pig's Eye' Parrant, the one-eyed bootlegger who had led squatters to the settlement.

Paul is a municipality on the island of Santo Antão, northernmost of the Cape Verde islands. It was colonised by the Portuguese in 1462 and sits in the Northern Atlantic off the west coast of Africa. Agriculture and tourism are Paul's main sources of income.

Paul is surrounded by endless blue ocean on one side and towering walls of lush, green valley on the other. The district has a total area of 54.26 km² and a population of just over 8,000. Portuguese, Africans, Spaniards, Italians, English and Americans have all settled there; the Africans as slaves until 1780 when Royal Decree declared the population of the island free.

St. Pauli is one of the 105 quarters of Hamburg, Germany and contains one of the world's most famous red light districts, 'The Reeperbahn'. Literally translated as 'the Rope Walk' it was home to the rope makers in the mid-17th century. The Beatles famously lived in St. Pauli and played at the Star Club before becoming famous.

Originally built in 604AD, **St. Paul's Cathedral** was rebuilt in 962 after a Viking ransacking. A fire in 1087 meant it had to be rebuilt once more and it took over 200 years to complete – finally in 1314. In 1666 the Great Fire of London decimated the roofs; Christopher Wren was instructed to rebuild the city. His first design was rejected, and the second abandoned. His third design was cleared; work began and was finished in 1710. St. Paul's is the second biggest dome in the world, after St. Peter's Basilica in Rome.

St. Paul's Cathedral's south-west tower houses Great Paul, the largest bell in the British Isles. Great Paul, rings out at 1pm every day, weighs 16½ tons and is larger than Big Ben. At 37,474 lbs, Great Paul stands at 32nd in the world listing. The Tsar Kolokol in Russia's Kremlin is the largest bell at a colossal 433,356 lbs.

St. Paul's Bridge in Astley Bridge, Bolton is set very close to the A666. Ghoulish.

French-owned **St. Paul Island (Île Saint-Paul)** is a tiny island in the Indian Ocean almost equidistant between the southern tip of Africa and the western southern tip of Australia. There is no permanent population due to an inactive volcano on the island. However, in 1928 a spiny lobster cannery was established there. In 1931, seven employees of the cannery were abandoned on the island when the company went bankrupt. As five died and two were finally rescued some three years later they became known as: Les Oubliés de Saint-Paul – 'the forgotten ones of St. Paul'.

Malta's **St. Paul's Island** is so called after, in 60AD, the Roman Governor of Palestine Porcius Festus allowed **Paul** of Tarsus passage to Rome to stand trial for heresy before the Emperor Nero. During his three-month stay on the island he sowed the first seeds of the Maltese people's Christian religion.

One of the four volcanic Pribof Islands located in the Bering Sea off the coast of Alaska, **Saint Paul Island** is the only inhabited one. It has one school, which serves 100 students, one post office, one bar, one small store, and one church, which is Russian Orthodox. The native peoples of the island are the Aleut tribe. Forced into slavery by the Russians, the Aleuts hunted, cleaned and prepared seal skins which the Russians sold on. A dwarf variety of woolly mammoth survived on the island until 6000 BC, the most recent survival of North American mammoth. The island is also the scene of the Rudyard Kipling story *The White Seal* and poem *Lukannon* in *The Jungle Book*.

Nicknamed 'The Graveyard of The Gulf', the desolate **St. Paul Island** is a small uninhabited place located approximately 24 km (15 miles) north-east of Cape North on Cape Breton Island and 71 km (44 miles) south-west of Cape Ray on Newfoundland. An extension of the Appalachian Mountains, the highest point is Croggan Mountain. The island's ecosystem is considered so fragile that visitors to the island must be cleared by the Canadian Coast Guard. Fog-bound throughout much of the navigation season, the island's light station is automated using solar power.

Saint Paul in Portuguese, **Sao Paulo** is Brazil's largest city with a population of almost 11 million, with up to almost 20 million in the metropolitan area. Including descendants, there are six million Italians who call Sao Paulo home. The city's Gay Parade is the biggest in the world, attracting over three million people. Its twin towns include Milan, Barcelona, Shanghai, Miami and Paris. It does not have a British twin town. In Brazil, where kissing on each cheek is commonplace, Sao Paulo is an exception – unmarried women often kiss a third time and mutter para casar 'to marry' – a charm designed to promote the chances of finding a husband.

First coming to prominence in 1615, **Paul** is a pleasant mountainside village seated near Covilha on the southern slope of the Estrela mountain range in Portugal, on the banks of the Caia River. **Paul** is marked by winding narrow streets, surrounded by small houses in agricultural areas. Lovely.

After the September 11th attack on New York's Twin Towers, for eight months, **St. Paul's Chapel** became a place of rest and refuge for recovery workers at the site. When the World Trade Center was hit, the church survived without even a broken window. Folklore decrees that it was spared by a single protective sycamore tree on the north-west corner hit by debris. The tree's root has been preserved in a bronze memorial by sculptor Steve Tobin.

GOOD SPORTS

England rugby winger **Paul Sackey** cites sprint coaching with Margot Wells, wife of the former Olympic 100 metres sprint champion Allan, as one of the reasons for his blistering pace.

Paul Hunter, aka the Beckham of the Baize, was a talented English professional snooker player markedly better looking than his pallid peers. His girlfriend clearly concurred. Following his 2001 Masters Title win, Hunter admitted to resorting to what he called 'Plan B' eight games into the final. At 6-2 down, during the interval, Hunter and girlfriend Lindsey Fell retired to their hotel room. Hunter confessed: "Sex was the last thing on my mind. I just wasn't in the mood. But I had to do something to break the tension. It was a quick session – around 10 minutes or so – but I felt great afterwards. She jumped in the bath; I had a kip and then played like a dream. I reeled off four centuries in six frames. I won easily."

The bowling action of South African bowler **Paul Adams** was famously likened to a 'frog in a blender' by England cricketer Mike Gatting. Adams was a Chinaman bowler; someone who bowls from the right hand side of the wicket using a left arm and spins into the body of the batsman.

Paul Runyan, a member of the World Golf Hall of Fame and double PGA Championship winner in 1934 and 1938, was nicknamed Little Poison because at 5ft 7ins he couldn't drive very far but had a killer short game.

English cricketer **Paul Collingwood MBE** – who played under-13s cricket when he was just nine – plays off a golf handicap of "five or six" and, on June 21st 2005 became the first player to score a century and take six wickets in a One Day International. Collingwood scored 112 not out from 86 balls and took six Bangladesh wickets for 31 runs.

Tennis pro **Paul Haarhuis** earned $7.5m over the course of his career despite a singles record that saw him win 267 and lose 258. Haarhuis was a doubles specialist who won six grand slam doubles titles.

Law Unto Themselves

Career criminal **Paul Baldwin** has been arrested 152 times. Upon his 152nd appearance in court, when asked if he would like a lawyer to represent him, he told Judge Sawako Gardner: "I've been in this court more than you have. I don't need a lawyer."

In 2004, lawyer **Paul Zellerbach** was reprimanded by a California state judicial agency for refusing to leave a Los Angeles Angels versus Boston Red Sox play-off game. Zellerbach was due back in court to hear the jury verdict in a double murder case.

THE MASTERS

Born in 1962, **Paul Motwani** was Scotland's first chess Grandmaster. He was a secondary school mathematics teacher in Dundee for a number of years after studying mathematics and physics at Dundee University.

Living between 1837 and 1884 American **Paul Morphy**, aka 'The Pride and Sorrow of Chess', is considered one of the greatest chess players ever. Growing up in New Orleans, one story tells how despite never being taught chess – he had been watching his father and uncle play intently for numerous summers – he told his father how the game should have been won. Morphy took all the pieces back and showed him. As a nine-year-old in 1846, he beat visiting General Winfield Scott, and at twelve Hungarian chess master Johann Lowenthal 3-0. Both opponents originally sneered at a contest with a child. Morphy would take on eight players at once while playing blindfold chess. After beating all the best players in the world while on tour in Europe, he hung up his board. The last 25 years of his life were chessless.

Estonian **Paul Keres**, who lived between 1916 and 1975, was dubbed 'The Crown Prince of Chess', another global phenomenon. Due to the Soviet occupation of Estonia during World War II, it is rumoured that Keres was forced to lose or draw important games against Soviet players to avoid deportation to Siberia. However, after the war, in 1947, 1950 and 1951 he won the formidable USSR Chess

Championship three times and between 1936 and 1965 he was never out of the world top ten. The five kroons Estonian banknote bears his portrait. In 2000, he was named the Estonian Sportsman of the Century. On why he never became world champion, Keres famously replied: "I was unlucky, like my country."

YANKEE(ISH) DOODLE PAULY SPORTSMEN

Chris Paul, 2006 NBA Rookie of the Year and Beijing
Olympics gold medal basketball player once, during a high
school game, scored 61 points in honour of his grandfather
who, only days before, was beaten to death in his own
carport during a robbery. Paul scored one point for every
year his grandfather lived. When Paul reached the 61-point
mark, he intentionally missed a free throw, and asked his
coach to take him out of the game. This, even though the
state high school scoring record of 69 points was well within
reach.

Famous American football coach **Paul William 'Bear'
Bryant** earned his nickname from wrestling a captive bear
during a theatre promotion as a 13-year-old.

Paul Stastny is the latest in a line of Stastnys to play in
the US National Hockey League. The lineage also includes
father Peter, the first European-trained player to reach
1,000 points in the NHL, older brother Yan and uncles
Marian and Anton. Paul is one of the few NHL players to
still use a wooden stick.

Canadian **Paul Henderson**, the left wing of ice
hockey's Detroit Red Wings 'HUM Line', along with
Norm Ullman, and Bruce MacGregor, is best known
for scoring the winning goal in the 1972 Summit Series
– the first competition between full-strength ice hockey

teams from Russia and Canada. With the teams at three wins each and one game drawn, and at 5-5 in the eighth game with the Soviets set to win on goal difference from the previous six games, there was 34 seconds remaining when Henderson took the ice. He skated straight towards the Russian net and scored "the goal heard around the world". It is remembered as the greatest moment in Canadian sporting history. Not remembered as a fantastic player, Henderson also scored the decisive goals in games six and seven!

Paul Rapier Richards, the famous Major League Baseball player, manager, scout and executive is responsible for designing the oversized catcher's glove used to catch knuckleball pitches. The knuckleball has an erratic, unpredictable motion due to the minimal spin of the ball in flight. It can sometimes even corkscrew, which makes the pitch difficult for batters to hit, pitchers to control and umpires to decide whether it was a strike or not.

Legendary baseball batter **Paul Glee Waner**, who played for the Pittsburgh Pirates in the twenties and thirties was nearsighted, a fact that Pirate management only learned late in his career when he remarked that he had difficulty reading the ads posted on the outfield walls. Fitting him with glasses, however, only interfered with his hitting, as Waner now had to contend with a small spinning projectile rather than the fuzzy grapefruit-sized object he had been hitting before.

American football quarterback **'Pitchin' Paul Christman**, a member of the Chicago Cardinals legendary 'Million Dollar Backfield', which led the Cardinals to the first NFL Championship in 1947, was a notoriously poor ball-handler and at one time owned the record for most fumbles in a game, five – it's now seven – and most own fumbles recovered in a season, eight – it's now 12. His daughter is noted Scientology critic Tory Christman.

A pinched nerve robbed quarterback **Paul Hornung** from leading the Green Bay Packers to victory in the first Super Bowl in 1967. Hornung was the first selection in the 1957 NFL Draft. In 1961, Hornung was called to active US Army duty but played on Sunday thanks to a weekend pass negotiated by famous coach Vince Lombardi, a close personal friend of then President John F. Kennedy.

YOU WANT THE TRUTH?!

NBA basketball's **Paul Anthony Pierce** is nicknamed
The Truth, following a post-match interview with imposing
centre/film star Shaquille O'Neal. After a 2001 Los Angeles
Lakers victory over the Boston Celtics, O'Neal told a
Boston reporter: "Take this down. My name is Shaquille
O'Neal and Paul Pierce is the motherfucking truth. Quote
me on that and don't take nothing out. I knew he could
play, but I didn't know he could play like this. Paul Pierce is
The Truth." On September 25th, 2000, Pierce was stabbed
11 times in the face, neck, and back while at the Buzz Club
in Boston. He had lung surgery to repair the damage before
playing all 82 games in the 2000/01 season.

PEN PAULS

"There's nothing in the world for which a poet will give up writing, not even when he is a Jew and the language of his poems is German"
Paul Celan's letter to relatives in 1948

"Poetry is a long word which can be stretched"
Paul Farley.

Celebrity journalist to just about everyone, **Paul Callan** is credited with the shortest interview ever published. Meeting the reclusive Greta Garbo at the Hotel du Cap Eden Roc near Cannes, Callan got as far as: "I wonder…" before Garbo cut in with, "Why wonder?", and stalked off. The story ran across a full page in the *Daily Mail.*

Author of *The Alchemist* **Paulo Coelho** was 38 when he published his first book.

Nicknamed 'The Professor of Pop', DJ **Paul Gambaccini** is a massive fan of comic books having had a fan letter published in the likes of *The Amazing Spiderman* as far back as the 1960s. In fact, Paul Gambi, a recurring character in *The Flash*, was based in homage to and on Gambaccini's physical appearance. Gambi was a tailor who produced the colourful costumes worn by the villains who fought The Flash.

The lead character in DH Lawrence's *Sons & Lovers*,
Paul Morel, is thought to be an autobiographical nod
to Lawrence's struggle to free himself from his own life.
Re-written four times by Lawrence, the book marks the
first modern portrayal of the Oedipus complex. Paul
is hopelessly devoted to his mother, and that love often
borders on romantic desire. It is coupled with a hatred of
his father that includes fantasies of murder. The book was
originally called Paul Morel but Lawrence changed the title
to take focus away from the central character, and himself.

The world's first supervillain may well have been *John Devil*,
created by one of the fathers of modern crime fiction **Paul
Henri Corentin Féval** in 1862. His novel *Jean Diable*
includes Scotland Yard Chief Superintendent *Gregory Temple*
who becomes mystified by the actions of a supremely gifted
crime leader who hides behind the name *John Devil*. Féval
also created one of the first crime fighters. *Les Habits Noirs*,
written over 12 years from 1863 to 1875, featured eleven
novels, the latter of which celebrated a heroic albino who
fights for justice in a *Zorro*-like disguise – one of the earliest
treatments of a crimefighter with a secret identity.

'The King of Soho', whose real name was Geoffrey
Anthony Quinn, (he obviously thought Paul gave him
greater gravitas), **Paul Raymond** was the owner and
creator of adult magazines *Razzle*, *Men Only* and *Mayfair*. He
opened Britain's first strip club, The Raymond Revuebar,
on April 21st 1958. In 2004 he was valued at £600 million,
just four years before he died.

Inflamer of German patriotism and shaper of public opinion to the will of the Nazis, **Paul Joseph Goebbels**, actually publicly abandoned the use of Paul. Joseph Goebbels earned a PhD in 1921, writing his doctoral thesis on 18th century romantic drama. However, he will be best remembered for his book-burning campaign which began in 1933 with the aim of removing any literature deemed "un-German". Towards the end of World War II, Goebbels remained with Hitler in Berlin to the very end. Following Hitler's suicide, his wife Magda killed their six young children before ending their own lives. He is rumoured to have had a club foot.

Charles Dickens' *Dombey and Son* is about a father and son, both called **Paul**. The father owns a shipping company and dearly wants his son to continue his business. The child is weak and often ill and is sent away to improve his health and schooling, but dies. He is just six years old and Paul senior must bond with his previously neglected daughter, Florence. The characters are thought to be based on Dickens' family. Fanny Dickens, Charles' oldest sister, had a crippled son, Henry Jr., who Dickens used as a model for Paul Dombey junior, and later *A Christmas Carol*'s Tiny Tim).

The novel ***Paul Clifford***, published in 1830 by Edward Bulwer-Lytton, tells of the life of the gentleman criminal. Immediately popular upon its release, *Paul Clifford* opens with seven words that have become among English literature's most famous references: "*It was a dark and stormy night*; the rain fell in torrents – except at occasional intervals, when it was checked by a violent gust of wind which swept up the streets (for it is in London that our scene lies), rattling along the housetops, and fiercely agitating the scanty flame of the lamps that struggled against the darkness."

The 'I' in *Withnail and I* (the 'I' character is actually called Marwood), **Paul McGann** became the eighth *Doctor Who* in 1996. He was originally cast to play ITV's *Sharpe* but broke his leg playing football a few days into the shooting and was replaced by Sean Bean. McGann's injury triggered, at the time, the largest insurance settlement in British television history – £2,128,172. On his *Doctor Who* career, he noted: "I don't want to be remembered as the George Lazenby of *Doctor Who*." Too late!

Paul of Aegina or Paulus Aegineta was a 7th century Byzantine Greek physician best known for writing the medical encyclopaedia *Medical Compendium in Seven Books*. For many years in the Byzantine Empire, this work contained the sum of all Western medical knowledge – it was unrivalled in its accuracy and completeness. The sixth book on surgery in particular was referenced in Europe and the Arab world right up to and through the Middle Ages and is of special interest for surgical history. The whole work in the original Greek language was published in Venice in 1528. Were proof needed of its impact and longevity consider that it was eventually translated into English around 1845.

Paul, the 2005 play by Howard Brenton, portrays the life and career of Paul the Apostle and was performed in the Lyttelton auditorium of the National Theatre, London from September 30th 2005 to February 4th 2006, in modern dress. The press night was postponed due to the exhaustion of the cast, whilst the National received 200 letters of complaint and outrage, on religious grounds, even before opening night.

On the letters of complaint, Theatre Director Nicholas Hytner noted: "They are all praying for me, and they are telling me I will go to hell unless I take the play off. I don't mind, because I don't believe in hell."

The main objections surrounded the fact that *Paul* a) portrayed Jesus as having survived the crucifixion and b) portrayed Jesus' appearance to Paul on the road to Damascus as an encounter engineered by Mary Magdalene and Peter and not the holy vision reported in the Bible.

Leading British gay journalist, broadcaster and author **Paul Burston** is co-curator of the House of Homosexual Culture at the South Bank Centre. In 2007 and 2008, he was included in *The Independent* newspaper's 1001 most influential gay people in Britain, aka *The Pink List*.

Do you want to lose weight? Do you want to become rich? Do you want to become more confident? Do you want to improve your life? Do you want to read lists of questions?

If you do, **Paul McKenna PhD**, "the World's leading hypnotist and an expert in the power of the human mind", is your man. McKenna is, according to *The Sunday Times* newspaper, Britain's best selling non-fiction author. The former in-store Radio Topshop DJ taught comedian David Walliams a 'time distortion technique' to help with his swim across the English Channel. McKenna is, according to his website, regularly watched on television by hundreds of millions of people in 42 countries. Couldn't he just beam into their minds?

There have been four authors called **Paul** to win a category in the *Whitbread Book Prize*, the award chosen by the Booksellers Association of Great Britain and Ireland. Since 2006, the awards were re-christened the *Costa Book Awards* after naming rights were taken over by Costa Coffee.

Paul Durcan won the 1990 Whitbread Poetry Prize for his poem *Daddy, Daddy*.
Durcan appeared on the Van Morrison album *Enlightenment*, giving an idiosyncratic vocal performance on the song *In The Days Before Rock 'n' Roll*, which he also co-wrote.

Paul Theroux, father of UK TV presenter Louis, won the 1978 Best Novel prize for *Picture Palace*. He was one of seven children, keeps bees and produces his own brand of honey. On the greatest piece of advice he's ever been given while travelling, he told *The Independent* newspaper: "You can go anywhere in the world, if you go slowly."

Paul Sayer won the 1988 *Whitbread Best First Novel* and *Book of the Year Prize* for *The Comforts of Madness*. In it Sayer draws on his experience as a staff nurse in a psychiatric hospital. Put simply, the plot is the unspoken monologue of Peter. Peter is catatonic. In fact, he hasn't moved for so long his bones are melding together, his intestines are gluing up and his sight is dwindling.

Paul Murray made the shortlist in 2003 for his book *An Evening of Long Goodbyes*. "Charles Hythloday is resolved to do absolutely nothing with his life. A twenty-something malcontent who rejects reality, he spends his days and nights watching Gene Tierney movies at his family's crumbling estate near Dublin and emptying the contents of its wine cellar."

⋙◆⋘

"The Japanese have perfected good manners and made them indistinguishable from rudeness"
Paul Theroux in *The Great Railway Bazaar*

FOODIE AND DRINKIE PAULS

It was *Observer* food writer **Paul Levy** who coined the phrase "foodie".

The Ulverston Brewing Company was started by **Paul Swann** and partner in 2006. After sitting a start-up course at The University of Sunderland, the pair has gone from a renovated shed to a thousand pints a week. Swann keeps a strong local connection; their beers Lonesome Pine, Another Fine Mess and Laughing Gravy are named after Laurel and Hardy films – Stan Laurel was born in Ulverston.

Paul Bocuse is one of the most prominent chefs associated with the nouvelle cuisine – the term was first used to describe the cuisine in a newspaper article during 1972 – which is less opulent and high-calorie than the traditional haute cuisine, and stresses the importance of fresh ingredients of the highest quality. In 1975, he created the world famous *soupe aux truffes* (truffle soup) for a presidential dinner at the Elysée Palace. Since then, the soup has been served in Bocuse's restaurant near Lyon as Soupe VGE, VGE being the initials of former president of France Valéry Giscard d'Estaing.

Take a trip to France and eat at **Paul**! The French bakery swung open its doors in 1889 in the city of Croix by Charlemagne Mayot. There over 300 Paul cafés franchised

from France to Japan, Spain to Dubai, Netherlands to
Lebanon. Paul opened its first bakeries in the US in 2006.
Paul specialises in serving over 140 types of bread, crepes,
sandwiches and cakes. Over 300 French farmers plant over
35 square kilometres (8,650 acres) for Paul. What started
out as a quaint little eaterie is now owned by Groupe
Holder in Lille. Progress, eh?

The self-proclaimed "Champagne King of California",
Paul Masson's first sparkling wine under the name
'champagne' was introduced at Almaden in 1892. Paul
Masson wine is well-remembered for its 1970s marketing
campaign in which Orson Welles promised: "We will sell no
wine before its time." An infamous outtake shows a Welles
who has clearly drank wine well before an advisable time.

Since 1987, the Bocuse d'Or, the brainchild of French chef
Paul Bocuse, has been regarded as the most prestigious
award for chefs in the world (at least when French food is
considered), and is sometimes seen as the Chef's Olympics.
The 2009 competition, held in Lyon, had to use:

- Angus fillet steak: 2 kg to 2.5 kg
- One oxtail: 1 kg
- Two ox cheeks: 500g per cheek
- Three beef ribs: 3 to 4 kg total, supplied not
  stripped

For fish, the chefs had to use:

- One piece Norwegian fresh cod: 5 to 6 kg, complete with its head
- Norwegian king scallops: 45 pieces with their shells (12-13cm)
- Norwegian wild prawns, uncooked: 3 kg

Paul – a name for rulers

Born in St. Petersburg in 1754, the Mad Tsar (is there a pattern emerging here?) **Paul I of Russia** succeeded his mother Catherine the Great in 1796, aged 41. His birth, death, paternal parentage and indeed life continue to be the subject of much debate. Peter the Great *and* Catherine's courtier Sergei Saltykov have both been linked with Paul's siring. Paul's relationship with his mother was an acidic one; he considered her the murderer of his father, she thought him stupid and ugly. While Catherine believed the Empire's peasants were there to facilitate her luxurious lifestyle, Paul believed in a more universal prosperity. It was an approach that did little to endear him to fellow Russian nobles. As Paul concluded (shortly before he was murdered by 'noble' conspirators on March 11th 1801): "I prefer to be hated for a rightful cause than loved for a wrong one."

Shortly before his reign between 1947 and 1964, **King Paul of Greece** was part of the government-in-exile that resided in London during the German occupation. Despite the hospitality and his being the cousin of Prince Philip, a little later links with Britain became strained over Cyprus, where the majority Greek population favoured union with the homeland. Britain, as the colonial power, could and would not endorse such a move. In 1960, Cyprus eventually became an independent state. Paul attracted criticism for the cost of maintaining the royal family. He responded by donating his private estate at Polidendri to the State.

Paulus Catena was a senior civil servant who served under the Roman Emperor Constantius II in the middle of the 4th century. Paulus was infamous for his unparalleled cruelty which earned him the nickname Catena (The Chain). Paulus had a predilection for chaining people and dragging them through the streets. In Britain he hunted down supporters of the recently-defeated commander of the Herculians Magnentius and went about doing so with vigour and abandon, often jailing at whim. In Egypt, he set up a kangaroo court and began summarily passing judgment on suspected traitors. He hunted down the followers of Frankish usurper Claudius Silvanus, torturing then killing them. In 362, Paulus was burned alive. If you live by the sword...

Stephanus Johannes Paulus Kruger, better known as **Paul Kruger** and to Afrikaans as 'Uncle Paul' was State President of the South African Republic and the face of the Boer resistance against the British during the South African or Second Boer War which ran between 1899 and 1902. Never far from his pipe, Kruger was an inveterate smoker. He was also known as Mamelodi'a Tshwane, "whistler of the Apies River", by the indigenous Tswana for his ability to whistle and imitate bird calls. The Krugerrand, the South African gold coin, is named after **Paul Kruger**, President of Transvaal – the north-eastern region of the country – from 1883 to 1899. What is not so public knowledge about the man is that in 1897 he believed the Earth to be flat.

Until 1806, the effigy burnt annually in England on November 5th was not Guy Fawkes but that of **Pope Paul V**. The Gunpowder Plot was an attempt by provincial English Catholics to kill James I of England and most of his Protestant aristocracy, at the State opening of Parliament on November 5th, 1605. Pope Paul V was seen by the English as having a controlling hand on the attempt on their King's life.

Pope Benedict declared a Jubilee Year to **St. Paul** which started on June 28th 2008 and continued until June 29th 2009 in celebration of the 2,000th anniversary of the saint's birth. A series of 13 banners, each standing over six feet high depicting the life of St Paul, are on display in the Chapel of St Paul in Westminster Cathedral.

Paul Kagame, the current President of Rwanda, was born to a Tutsi family in 1957. At the age of three, Kagame and his family fled to Uganda to avoid slaughter by Rwanda's revolting Hutu faction. In 1979, aged just 22, Kagame returned to lead the Rwandan Patriotic Army (RPA) in The Rwanda Civil War and liberated the Tutsi minority from the Hutu's violent rule. The origins of the conflict are largely a matter of opinion rather than fact. It is largely agreed that the Tutsi's conquered the Hutu in or around the 14th century due to their taller physical stature. This tribal dispute is more dormant than settled.

POLITICAL PAULS (AROUND THE WORLD) FROM CIA FACTBOOK OF WORLD LEADERS*

Paul Magnette
Belgium's Minister for Health, Social Action and Equal
Chances/Climate and Energy
Paulo Bernardo
Brazilian Minister of Planning and Budget
Paul Biya
President of Cameroon
Paul Nji Atanga
Cameroon Minister of Commerce
Paul Otto
Central African Republic Minister of Justice
Paul Mbot
Republic of Congo Minister of Security and Public Order
Paul Bouabre
Ivory Coast Minister of Planning and Development
Paul Abessole
Gabon Deputy Prime Minister
Paul Toungui
Gabon Minister of State for Economy, Finance, Budget, &
Privatization
Paul Biyoghe
Gabon Minister of State for Trade & Industrial
Development
Paul Acquah
Governor, Bank of Ghana
Paul Bien-Aime
Haiti Minister of Interior & Territorial Collectivises
Paul Gallagher
Ireland, Attorney General

Paul Otuoma
Kenya, Minister for Fisheries Development
Paulo Garrido
Mozambique, Minister of Health
Paulo Zucula
Mozambique, Minister of Transport & Communication
Paulius Matane
Papua New Guinea, Governer General
Paul Tiensten
Papua New Guinea, Minister for National Planning &
District Development
Paul Pacuraru
Romania, Minister of Labor, Social Solidarity, & Family
Paul Kagame
Rwanda President
Paul Badji
Senegal, Permanent Representative to the UN, New York
Paulo Conteh
Sierra Leone, Minister of Defense & National Security
Paul Chiu
Taiwan, Vice President, Executive Yuan (Vice Premier)
Paul Karalus
Tonga, Minister of Civil Aviation, Marine, & Ports
Paul Gopee-Scoon
Trinidad & Tobago, Minister of Foreign Affairs
Paul Murphy
UK, Secretary of State for Wales
Paul Mangwana
Zimbabwe, Minister of State Affairs Responsible for Land
& Resettlement Programs

September 2008

TWO PHOTOGRAPHERS NAMED PAUL

American photographer **Paul Outerbridge Jr.**, who worked throughout the first half of the 20th century, was noted for early use and experiments in colour photography. His work, particularly nude women, was reproduced in *Vanity Fair* and *Vogue* magazines just a year after he took his first pictures. His philosophy: "Art is life seen through man's inner craving for perfection and beauty – his escape from the sordid realities of life into a world of his imagining."

Modernist American photographer and filmmaker **Paul Strand** helped establish photography as an art form in the 20th century. He was described as "subversive" by successive American governments and although never officially a member of the Communist Party, many of his associates were either members or prominent socialist writers.

Seven architects named Paul

Born in France in 1938, **Paul Andreu** is best known for having planned numerous airports worldwide, notably; Manila, Jakarta, Shanghai Pudong, Abu Dhabi, Dubai, Cairo, Brunei, and Charles de Gaulle, which he has been in charge of planning and constructing since 1967. However, it has not all been plain sailing. On May 23rd 2004, a portion of Terminal 2E's ceiling collapsed, killing four people. Andreu blamed the collapse on poor execution by the building companies.

American **Paul Rudolph**, former Dean at the Yale School of Architecture, was known for cubist designs and highly complex floor plans, including the Yale Art and Architecture Building – a Brutalist structure which uses striking repetitive angles and geometries. As well as designing the incredible Wisma Dharmala Sakti office tower and the Lippo Centre in Hong Kong, Rudolph is most closely associated with a one-storey Sarasota house built on posts and complete with a concave roof to allow rainwater to drain off.

Belgian **Paul Saintenoy** was the son of an architect and began studying the family business in Antwerp in 1881. At the end of World War I, Saintenoy was appointed a member of the Royal Commission of Monuments and Sites and charged with rebuilding Belgium. His most significant work is now Brussels' Musical Instrument Museum. A mix of art nouveau, glass and steel, it was designed and opened as a department store.

One of Hitler's key architects, **Paul Schmitthenner**, formed, with **Paul Bonatz**, the architectural style of the Stuttgart School. Schmitthenner's maxim Schönheit ruht in Ordnung (beauty lies in geometric order) was an opponent of modern architects like Walter Gropius. For Schmitthenner, Goethe's beautiful garden cottage at Weimar was the ideal type of German residential building.

Paul Bonatz favoured a simplified neo-Romanesque style which can be seen in the design of Stuttgart Railway Station or Basel Art Museum. He openly criticised the renovation of the Royal Square in Munich by Paul Troost (Walter Gropius' colleague). He could have picked a better opponent; Troost was Hitler's architectural mentor and personal friend.

Born in 1878, **Paul Troost** was Adolf Hitler's favourite architect. Troost advocated a restrained, sparse approach, devoid of ornament and publicly railed against the art nouveau movement that preceded his work. His philosophy was echoed by his appearance; he was a tall, shaven-headed, bespectacled, academic-looking fellow.

In 1933, Troost began work on the Haus der Deutschen Kunst (House of German Art) in Munich which was to be a showpiece of Nazi painting and sculpture, and which became an icon of Nazi architecture. Its construction and eventual completion were accompanied by huge publicity, where it was always described as Hitler's work. Troost couldn't refute the claim; he would die in 1934, three years before the museum's grand opening – but his contribution remained.

In 1921, former orphan **Paul Williams** became one of his country's first certified African American architects. He was known as an outstanding draughtsman who perfected the skill of drawing upside down so that his clients, who may have been uncomfortable sitting next to a black architect, would see the drawings right side up. Williams designed more than 2,000 homes; most famously the house used for exterior scenes of the Colby mansion on TV show *The Colbys* and properties for Frank Sinatra.

"Planning is thinking beforehand how something is to be made or done, and mixing imagination with the product – which in a broad sense makes all of us planners." **Paul Williams**.

PAULS WHO SPENT TOO MUCH TIME WITH THEIR HEADS IN BOOKS (LIKE YOU)

Paul Samuelson was, in 1970, the first American to receive the Nobel Prize for Economics and the first economist to try and define public good. The *Lindahl-Bowen-Samuelson Condition* is an equation that establishes whether an action will improve social welfare. The most easy-to-understand part of the theory (and there's a lot of it) says that when private and public provisions are substituted for one another, society becomes less happy. For example, he says that public goods you have to have (street-lighting, policing, defence etc.) cannot be supplied by the free market where provision of a service or product is contingent on payment. Also, because there is no need for competition to provide street lighting, it would be inefficient to charge for its consumption. He's too clever for me too.

Insect pests clearly upset **Paul Leary**, one of the world's foremost experts on insect pests in buildings. Leary gets lairy on his website, proclaiming: "Insect pests are responsible for the continual, often undetected, erosion of our cultural heritage and the undermining of the structural integrity of many of our significant architectural masterpieces." What an aerosol.

Paul Jardetzky was, along with a group of other University of Cambridge students, the creator of the world's webcam. The webcam had an extremely important use – it was pointed at a coffee pot to save students from a

pointless trip to the coffee room when the pot was empty.
Connected in 1993, it was switched off in 2001.

Paul Winchell patented a design for the artificial heart in
the mid-1950s. However, it wasn't until December 1st 1982,
at the University of Utah Medical Center in Salt Lake City,
that Dr William C. DeVries implanted dentist Dr Barney
Clark with a Jarvik-7, an artificial heart designed by Robert
Jarvik. Clark survived for 112 days. That, however, is not
how Winchell will be remembered. Winchell was, until
1999, also the voice of Tigger in *Winnie the Pooh*, Boomer in
The Fox and the Hound, the Siamese cat in Disney's *Aristocats*
and evil Gargamel from *The Smurfs*.

Paul Adolph Volcker is an American economist best
known as Chairman of the US Federal Reserve under
Jimmy Carter and Ronald Reagan. Today the 6ft 7ins New
Jersey native is an economic advisor to Barack Obama. Avid
fisherman Volcker once recounted: "The greatest strategic
error of my adult life was to take my wife to Maine on our
honeymoon on a fly-fishing trip."

INSERT YOUR OWN PUNCHLINE AT THE BOTTOM

A New York woman was cured, through brain surgery, after suffering grand mal seizures nearly every time she listened to her favourite musician **Sean Paul**.

———⊰◆⊱———

BUTTERFLIGHT OF FANCY

Paul Ralph Ehrlich is a renowned entomologist specialising in Lepidoptera – butterflies. However, he's keen on a prediction or two on the fate of human population, perhaps extrapolated from his flights of fancy? In 1969 he suggested: "By 1980 the United States would see its life expectancy drop to 42 because of pesticides, and by 1999 its population would drop to 22.6 million" and "I would take even money that England will not exist in the year 2000." On Earth Day 1970, he proclaimed: "In ten years all important animal life in the sea will be extinct. Large areas of coastline will have to be evacuated because of the stench of dead fish."

Pauls who give giggle

Paul Calf, created from the warped mind of Steve Coogan, is an unemployed Mancunian waster with a particular hatred of students whose approach to the world can be best summed up by his catchphrase "bag of shite". Calf lives in a council house in the fictional town of Ottle with his mother and his sister, Pauline (also played by Coogan). Obsessed with getting back with his ex-girlfriend, Julie, who later married his best friend Fat Bob, Paul is a Manchester City supporter who loves Wagon Wheels, wears Burton suits, sports a bleached mullet and drives a Ford Cortina.

Better known as **Paul Merton** (after the district where he grew up), Paul James Martin's comedic style, a monologue of increasingly improbable and surreal scenarios, alongside the straightest of faces, was reportedly inspired by watching circus clowns as a boy. He failed his eleven plus, received an unclassified grade for metalwork at CSE and worked at the Tooting Employment Office. His first professional comedic appearance was as a yokel in *The Young Ones*. Merton booked himself into the Maudsley psychiatric hospital after he was hallucinating conversations with friends, and became convinced he was a target for the Freemasons. Were proof needed of his insanity, he nearly took over as host of *Countdown*.

Comedian **Paul Betney** has a form of sclerosis which makes him shake incessantly. He is a regular member of comedy troupe 'Abnormally Funny People'.

At the age of eight, chirpy street magician, now *Countdown* regular, **Paul Zenon** conned his neighbours into buying raffle tickets for a non-existent prize then invented a fictional winner so they wouldn't catch on. He worked his way around the Mediterranean as a street magician, fire-eater and phoney fortune-teller, then as a casino croupier in Denmark. Zenon is also the founder of The Wonderbus, a not-for-profit organisation which takes older people on days out to see live entertainment.

Born in Glamorgan, Wales, **Paul Whitehouse** moved to Essex when he was four-years-old, which led to him discovering his talent for impersonations – he didn't speak at his new school for the first four weeks for fear of ridicule. His first words were reportedly: "Muumm, I wanna go to Sarfend!" He and Charlie Higson were inspired to write comedy after working as tradesmen on a house shared by Hugh Laurie and Stephen Fry. They met Harry Enfield in a local pub – Whitehouse would later create *Stavros* and *Loadsamoney* for Enfield. Johnny Depp has described Whitehouse as one of the best actors he has seen.

Australian Golden Globe-winning actor and comedian, **Paul Hogan**, was born in 1939. His Channel Four show, of which 60 were produced, went out on a Friday night and were British cult viewing in the early 1980s. Hogan was a rigger working on the Sydney Harbour Bridge before rising to fame in the early 1970s after a comical interview on news programme *A Current Affair*. Hogan's first film *Crocodile Dundee* was privately funded by Hogan and a group of investors including much of its cast, entrepreneur Kerry Packer, and cricketers Greg Chappell, Dennis Lillee, and Rod Marsh. It became the most successful Australian film ever and won him a Golden Globe Award for Best Actor in a Comedy.

Self-proclaimed black ringmaster, **Paul Mooney** grew up in California and landed his first professional work as a writer for Richard Pryor on *Saturday Night Live* and *Live on the Sunset Strip*. As head writer for *The Richard Pryor Show*, he gave Robin Williams and Sandra Bernhard their big breaks. He also created the character Homey D. Clown, played by Damon Wayans. In September 2005, Mooney performed a segment at the 2005 BET Comedy Awards called the "Nigga Wake Up Call Award".

In it Mooney mocked Diana Ross for drink driving. When accused of his 'attack' being over the top, he replied: "How can somebody get arrested for drink driving and go to jail and I be over the top? I think that's over the top, don't you?" During a 2006 performance at the Apollo Theatre Mooney made several jokes about Bush looking like the devil and one stating that his mother looked like the "guy on the Quaker Oats box". He was immediately pulled from the stage due, allegedly, to Time Warner intervention.

Comedian **Paul O'Grady MBE**, previously known as Lily Savage, has previously been a civil servant, barman for Yates's Wine Lodge, office worker in an abattoir, woodsman and assistant clerk at Liverpool Magistrates' Court. Openly

gay, O'Grady was once married to a Portuguese woman
and had a daughter, Sharyn. Listed at 32 in *The Independent*'s
2006 most influential gay men and women in Britain,
he is neighbours with Julian Clary. O'Grady got his idea
for Savage while working as a waiter in a bar/brothel in
Manila, Philippines.

PAUL IN THE URBAN DICTIONARY

The urban dictionary is the dictionary written – at random and whim – by the world at www.urbandictionary.com.

Paul (verb)
To mess something up or to make a bad situation worse.

USAGE
"Things were going well until you came and Pauled things up."

Paul (verb)
To get drunk then try shaving your balls, but in the process cutting the sack.

USAGE
"Oh fuck! I just Pauled my nuts!"

Paul (pronoun)
Someone who goes into a movie theatre and records the movie, then turns in the video as his own project in TV class.

USAGE
"Hey just Paul it and copy a movie."

Paul Bourglaised (verb/noun/adj.)
To get screwed over.

USAGE
*"Yo egg, if you went down the street you could have got that T-Shirt for half that price. You just got **Paul Bourgelaised**, big time."*

Paul (verb)
The act of penis insertion based solely on the female's nation of origin in order to effectively copulate with the whole world. Females are generally considered honoured to fornicate with such an individual.

USAGE
"Scott had never met a girl from India before, he couldn't wait to Paul her."

Paul
Your typical male in most cases, yet is all talk and no action.

USAGE
"That boy you're seeing, he's totally hot! Is he as good as he looks? Anna: "Yeah, he is hot! But he's such a Paul; I doubt I'll ever find out how good he really is!""

Paul (verb)
To miss the toilet and urinate on the surrounding ground. To have mechanical work done only to have it miss the mark on workmanship.

USAGE:
"Damn dude, you Pauled all around that toilet. Hey homes man, you really Pauled up that engine job."

"...AND IT'S PAUL UNITED, PAUL UNITED FC – THE GREATEST NAME THE WORLD HAS EVER SEEN..."

If there were a World Cup of names that ran throughout history, surely **Paul United** would be amongst the favourites. Have a look at this formidable starting line-up. Is there another name with as much outrageous footballing talent? We've gone for an 3-4-1-2 formation for all-out attack.

1	**Paul Cooper**	Ipswich Town
2	**Paul Reaney**	Leeds United & England
3	**Paolo Maldini**	AC Milan & Italy
4	**Paul McGrath**	Aston Villa & Ireland
5	**Paul Ince**	Manchester United & England
6	**Paul Gascoigne**	Tottenham Hotspur & England
7	**Pavel Nedved**	Juventus & Czech Republic
8	**Paul Scholes**	Manchester United & England
9	**Paul Breitner**	B. Munich & Germany
10	**Paulo Rossi**	Juventus & Italy
11	**Paul Merson**	Arsenal & England

Five-time Czech Player of the Year, **Pavel Nedvěd** is his country's most revered footballing name. Breaking through in Euro 96, he holds the record for scoring the last ever European Cup Winners' Cup goal (in 1999) before the competition was disbanded.

He joined Juventus in 2001 for $41 million (£32m) as a replacement for Zinedine Zidane and won four Italian titles, or Scudettos, in 2002, 2003, 2005 and 2006. He also won the 2003 'Ballon D'Or' (European Footballer of the

Year award) becoming the first Czech to do so. He's got a nasty side too. In 2006 Nedved broke Inter midfielder Luis Figo's fibula, a tackle for which he received a great deal of negative publicity.

FC St. Pauli football club has earned a cult following among German supporters – particularly left-leaning – thanks to its unique actions and philosophy. St. Pauli became the first team in Germany to officially ban right-wing, nationalist activities and displays in its stadium in an era when fascist-inspired football hooliganism threatened the game. The club has also been active in terms of charity. In 2005 the team and the fans initiated the "viva con agua de Sankt Pauli campaign" which collects money for water dispensers for schools in Cuba. The skull and crossbones has become the unofficial emblem of St. Pauli supporters across Germany.

Can you believe Chelsea paid £13.2million for **Paulo Ferreira**? Us neither.

The son of Kenny Dalglish, **Paul Dalglish** won the MLS Cup with Houston Dynamos in 2006 and 2007 before opening his 'Braveheart Soccer Camp'.

After a career playing for the likes of Chelsea, Birmingham and Queens Park Rangers **Paul Furlong** finally earned an international cap. Furlong turned out for

England C, the recently adopted moniker for the England non-league team.

The defensive half of a twin brother duo alongside centre-forward Ron, **Paul Futcher** was the most expensive defender in England when Manchester City signed him for £350,000 in 1978. He was twice picked to play for England; incredibly on both occasions he was involved in a road accident that prevented him from taking the pitch.

Paul Ince – the first black captain of England and one of the few English players to succeed in Italy – is best remembered for enraging supporters of West Ham United. In 1989 Ince was photographed wearing a Manchester United kit while still a Hammer. Appearing in the *Daily Express*, Ince received hatemail from West Ham fans for years. Ince explained the real reason for the faux pas in *FourFourTwo Magazine*:

"I spoke to Alex Ferguson and the deal was close to being done. I then went on holiday, and my agent at the time, Ambrose Mendy, said it wasn't worth me coming back to do a picture in a United shirt when the deal was completed, so I should do one before I left, and it would be released when the deal was announced. Lawrence Luster of the *Daily Star* took the picture and put it in the library. Soon after, their sister paper, the *Daily Express*, were looking for a picture of me playing for West Ham, and found the one of me in the United shirt in the pile. They published it and all hell broke loose. I came back from holiday to discover West Ham fans were going mad. It wasn't really my fault. I was only a kid; I did what my agent told me to do, then took all the crap for it."

Gillingham chairman **Paul Scally** bought £6m worth of fixtures and fittings for the club's Priestfield stadium for £600,000 from the Millennium Dome. He bought Gillingham for £1 in 1995 after becoming wealthy through the sale of a photocopying business. Prior to buying the Gills he was a Millwall supporter.

Nottingham Forest's mercurial and blonde-haired former winger **Paul McGregor** hung up his quicksilver boots at just 29 to pursue a career in music. McGregor is the lead singer of rock, black metal, indie, techno band Ulterior. Their sound is a challenging mix of uncompromising thrash overladen with echoey political and social indignation. He has abandoned his Paul roots, instead opting for the stage name 'Honey'.

Paul Jones, the former Wolverhampton Wanderers and Southampton goalkeeper, changed his name from Paul Quentins by deed poll in 1997 due to a family disagreement.

Paul Gascoigne, better known as Gazza, suffered personal tragedy as a boy, witnessing the death of Steven Spraggon, the younger brother of a friend, who was knocked down and killed by a car outside a sweet shop. At the age of 17, after advice from Gascoigne, friend Steven Wilson quit Middlesbrough and was about to sign forms with Newcastle. However, while waiting for the opening at Newcastle, Wilson was a victim of a fatal accident while working with his father on a building site.

One-club Italian footballer **Paolo Maldini** is the most-selected player in the history of AC Milan, Serie A and the Italy. Maldini made his league debut in 1985 aged just sixteen and in 2008, as a substitute against Parma, reached 1,000 senior games with Milan and Italy. With seven league titles, five Champions League titles and 126 caps for Italy, he is amongst the most decorated and respected players in the game's history. Milan have retired his famous number three shirt, but it will be bequeathed to one of his sons if they make the club's senior side. His eldest son, Christian, is twelve and currently plays for the Milan youth squad.

Paolo Rossi may have led Italy to the 1982 FIFA World Cup title – scoring six goals to win the Golden Boot and the Golden Ball, as the tournament's most valuable player, (the only player to win all three titles at a single tournament) – but his career will always be shrouded in scandal. At Perugia he was involved in a famous 'Totonero' match-fixing debacle, for which he was banned from playing for three years. He returned just in time for Espana '82 in poor shape and was labelled a ghost by journalists. His hat-trick against Brazil in the second round remains legendary.

Capped 48 times for his country, **Paul Breitner** was one of Germany's most controversial, yet successful, players. 'Afro-Paule' claimed to read Lenin and Marx; had himself photographed sat beneath a poster of Mao Tse-Tung; said that listening to the national anthem before international matches "ruins the concentration"; and went on strike just before the 1974 World Cup, successfully demanding a bonus of 100,000 DM per player if they won the trophy. However, he sold out, when agreeing, in 1982, to a deal with a German cosmetics company that offered to pay him 150,000 DM if he shaved off his characteristic fluffy beard, used their fragrance and advertised for the company.

THE TEN BEST PAUL CLIPS ON YOUTUBE

Pablo Francisco on gay gangs, killer Gary Busey and a
Danny Glover impression:
http://uk.youtube.com/watch?v=kCAwd-
J5fow&feature=related

Tony v **Paul** – killer stop-motion short:
http://uk.youtube.com/watch?v=AJzU3NjDikY

Cody Paul – killer running back:
http://uk.youtube.com/watch?v=fqSV1wnN5oQ

Paul Gilbert – killer guitar:
http://uk.youtube.com/watch?v=HC60XNiS-MQ

Paul Oakenfold Ready Steady Go – killer video:
http://uk.youtube.com/watch?v=aaVtjGfpmlo

Paul McCartney's Makes Mashed Potatoes:
http://uk.youtube.com/watch?v=WyyEc-GNDfQ

Paul Hunt gymnastics. Toe-curlingly embarrassing
comedy beam routine:
http://uk.youtube.com/watch?v=EO_BnsrWMnI

Paul Weller plays That's Entertainment with Noel Gallagher:
http://uk.youtube.com/watch?v=H4b48Jx7Un0

Paul Whitehouse – The Football Manager:
http://uk.youtube.com/watch?v=03Tck7-
1Ooc&feature=related

Paul Otlet conceives the Internet in 1934!
http://uk.youtube.com/watch?v=P0Y-
28M1Nto&feature=related

PAUL ON THE BIG SCREEN

Paul Verhoeven, the Dutch film director, whose trademark sexual/violent flicks include *Basic Instinct*, *Robocop* and *Total Recall*, could well have been scarred by the burning houses and bodies he experienced during WW2 in The Hague. He also claims to have seen the 1953 incarnation of *War of the Worlds* ten times. He is the only director to show up to collect a Golden Raspberry, awarded to the worst movie of the year, for his film *Showgirls*. He is a member of the Jesus Seminar, a secular organisation committed to the non-religious study of the life of Jesus Christ.

Actor **Paul Scofield**, who died in March 2008, refused a knighthood on three separate occasions, saying he wanted to remain "plain mister". He commented: "If you want a title, what's wrong with Mr? If you have always been that, then why lose your title? But it's not political. I have a CBE, which I accepted very gratefully."

He, along with Yul Brynner, Joel Grey, Rex Harrison, Anne Bancroft, Shirley Booth, Jose Ferrer and Jack Albertson, is one of just eight actors to win both an Academy Award and a Tony Award for the same role on film and stage; *A Man For All Seasons*. As a Brighton schoolboy he played Juliet in a school play.

Paul Lukas, the 1943 Oscar winner for his role as Kurt Muller in *Watch on the Rhine*, was born in Budapest, Hungary. Lukas moved to Hollywood in 1927 as a 36-year-old and became a US citizen in 1933 upon receipt of his Academy Award.

1951 Oscar winner **Paul Dehn**, who collected his golden man for *Seven Days to Noon*'s original screenplay, also wrote the *Planet of Apes*' four sequels: *Beneath the Planet of the Apes* (1970), *Escape from the Planet of the Apes* (1971), *Conquest of the Planet of the Apes* (1972) and *Battle for the Planet of the Apes* (1973).

Paul Giamatti, who played Nick 'Santa' Claus in the movie *Fred Claus*, doesn't celebrate Christmas. "My wife is Jewish so we celebrate Hanukkah," he confirmed.

Paul Francis Webster, inducted into the US Songwriters' Hall of Fame in 1972, won three Oscars for the films: *Secret Love* (1953), *Love is a Many Splendored Thing* (1955) and *The Shadow of your Smile* (1965). He was nominated an incredible 16 times. More recently he wrote his finest work: *Spider Pig* from *The Simpson's Movie*.

Paul Andrew Williams, who wrote Britflick *London to Brighton* and directed Brit horror *The Cottage,* has been linked with directing the superfluous *Lethal Weapon 5*.

Paul Levitz was the creator of *Barb Wire*, the bad girl played by Pamela Anderson in the film of the same name. *Barb Wire* was part of an attempt by Dark Horse Comics – creators of *Hellboy* and *The Mask* – to build a 'universe' of characters.

Paul Frees, aka The Man of a Thousand Voices, was, in the 1950s and 1960s, often called upon to re-loop the dialogue of other actors. This was most often to correct for foreign accents or a complete lack of English proficiency. These dubs often extended from single lines to entire roles. He is heard on four occasions in the 1960 film *Spartacus*, starring Kirk Douglas. It is his voice, not the actor's, that cries out when hamstrung by Douglas in the opening sequence.

Paul Thomas Anderson, the director of *There Will Be Blood* is considered one of the finest of his generation. He had an interesting grounding; his father Ernie used to host horror shows in his native Cleveland, USA under the pseudonym Ghoulardi. He went to New York University film school but decided to leave after handing in the work of Pulitzer Prize winner David Mamet and pretending he had produced it. It received a 'C'.

Paul Reiser, the cowardly company man Burke in *Aliens* made $1m an episode for the 1999 season of the American sitcom *Mad About You* opposite Helen Hunt.

1969 French flick ***Paul*** sees the eponymous lead leave his wealthy parents to go on a spiritual quest. He meets up with Yvan, the leader of a vegetarian cult whose members survive by begging for food. The religious fanatics are arrested for stealing eggs. Yvan butchers a goat and has a carnivore carnival orgy on the meat. Paul and Marianne, one of the followers, go to a remote island to live off seaweed and vegetation, but a development company wrecks the paradise. Paul is broken-hearted when Marianne goes off with one of the greedy developers. *Carry On Paul* it is not.

Last Stop for Paul (2006)
Charlie and Cliff decide they want to go to the Full Moon party in Thailand. Along the way they travel around the world sprinkling the ashes of their dead friend Paul.

Peter and Paul (1981)
Anthony Hopkins as **Paul** or Tarsus! Peter and Paul assume leadership of the church as they struggle against violent opposition to the teachings of Christ and their own personal conflicts.

Paul Gleason, the hard-nosed teacher in *The Breakfast Club*, attended and played football at Florida State University along with fellow actors Burt Reynolds and Robert Urich.

Paul Greengrass – he of *Bourne Ultimatum* headache-inducing shaky camera and rotund Billy Connolly lookalike – was the co-author of *Spycatcher*, the book which the British Government attempted to ban in 1987 for revealing

MI5 secrets. On his pre-film career working on ITV documentary series *World in Action*, Greengrass described it as: "A festival of puerile self-importance, intense paranoia, fiddled expenses and brilliant creativity."

Paul Dano played the sullen brother in *Little Miss Sunshine* and the boy-preacher in *There Will Be Blood*. Dano impressed Daniel Day-Lewis so much in the film *The Ballad of Jack and Rose* (in which Lewis and Dano appeared) that Lewis actually suggested him to *There Will Be Blood* director **Paul Thomas Anderson** when casting for the role of twins Paul and Eli Sunday. Dano is in a rock band called Mook.

Paul Walker, the blue-eyed hunky type who played opposite the equally adept thespian Vin Diesel in the noisiest film in cinema history, *The Fast and the Furious* and sequel *2 Fast 2 Furious*, also appeared in the teen time-travel flick, *Timeline*. His reported salary for *Timeline* was $3m; *2 Fast 2 Furious* $7m. Walker auditioned for the role of Anakin Skywalker in *Star Wars Episode I: The Last Hope* but was too old for the part.

Paul Schrader, writer on De Niro's *Taxi Driver*, *The Last Temptation of Christ* and *Raging Bull* was raised a strict Calvinist. So much so, he claims the first film he ever saw was, as an 18-year-old, Jerry Lewis' *The Nutty Professor*.

Paul Wing, winner of the 1935 Oscar for Assistant Director on the film *The Lives of a Bengal Lancer*, was one of the survivors of the 1942 Bataan Death March. The Bataan Death March saw the forcible 60-mile transfer of 75,000 American and Filipino prisoners of war captured by the Japanese during World War II. The march saw the Japanese commit beheadings, cut throats, casual shootings, bayonet stabbings, rapes, disembowelments, rifle-butt beatings and not allow food or water. Wing was subsequently also one of 513 prisoners of the Japanese prisoner of war camp Cabanatuan, portrayed in the 2005 film *The Great Raid*.

In 2005 **Paul Haggis** became the first person in history to write back-to-back Oscar winners; *Million Dollar Baby* and *Crash*. He had a heart attack while filming *Crash* but refused to let anyone else finish the film, instead returning to direct it two weeks after the incident. He also wrote Bond flick *Casino Royale* and penned episodes for *Diff'rent Strokes*.

Better known as his alter ego Pee Wee Herman, **Paul Reubens** was a former Marine. He was arrested in 1991 and charged with indecent exposure while viewing the adult film *Nurse Nancy*. He was the voice of Max in the film *Flight of the Navigator* and the father of Danny Devito, aka the Penguin, in *Batman Returns*. He is a committed collector of fake food.

Actor **Paul Newman** (b. 1925) made an inauspicious start to adulthood, getting expelled from Ohio University after just one year. On his eighteenth birthday, he enlisted in the Navy and later served as radioman/gunner on a torpedo plane in the Pacific during World War II. However, he was unable to complete his training as a US Navy pilot because of colour blindness.

He had, on the upside, his face on salad dressing bottles; the food company Newman's Own donated all post-tax profits and royalties to charity. It's thought these donations exceeded $250m. Newman finished second in the 1979 Le Mans 24-hour race in a Porsche 935. He was the co-founder of the Newman-Haas Nascar racing team and passed away on 26th September 2008 after a complicated illness arising from lung cancer.

The name of actor **Paul Newman** was discovered on President Richard Nixon's Enemies List, revealed in the aftermath of Watergate. The twenty-strong list was a collection of Nixon's political opponents.

Paul Newman started up The Hole In The Wall Camps for children with life-threatening illnesses. On the reason why, he noted: "I wanted to acknowledge luck: the chance and benevolence of it in my life, and the brutality of it in the lives of others, who might not be allowed the good fortune of a lifetime to correct it."

He thought his first film, *The Silver Chalice* (1954), so bad that Newman took out a full-page advertisement in a trade paper apologising to anyone who might have seen it. The rest of his career fared a little better. Newman was nominated on ten occasions for Academy Awards, including eight times as Best Actor, once as Best Supporting Actor, and once for Best Picture. In the acting category only Jack Nicholson (12 nominations – 8 Best Actor and 4 Best Supporting Actor) and Laurence Olivier (9 Best Actor and 1 Best Supporting Actor) have received more nominations.

He is godfather to *Brokeback Mountain* and *Donny Darko*'s Jake Gyllenhaal.

Actor **Paul Bettany** (b. 1971) was a former Westminster busker. He dropped out of school at 16 and spent the next two years as a London street performer. After a year working at a home for the elderly, he enrolled in drama school and made his debut in the West End revival of *An Inspector Calls*. His first exposure on American cinema screens came in *A Knight's Tale* where he played muddy, naked English poet Geoffrey Chaucer. "My buttocks entered the American market before I did," confirmed Bettany on the film's DVD. He met his future wife, Jennifer Connelly, on the set of *A Dangerous Mind* and has also played an Albino monk, in *The Da Vinci Code*.

Paul Edney is a member of the island survivor background cast of *Lost*; he plays an unnamed 'redshirt'. A redshirt is the industry term for a background character destined to die. Its origin lies in the *Star Trek*'s security officers who wore red shirts. Edney appears to specialise in small background roles as an extra, especially involving the military. His credits also include *Mission: Impossible III* (2006), *Ocean's Thirteen* (2007) and *Spiderman 3* (2007).

Veteran **Paul Sorvino** (b. 1939) has acted in around 100 films, most notably as Paul Cicero in *Goodfellas* and Henry Kissinger in *Nixon*. However, he's also an accomplished tenor, having sung with the Seattle Opera Company and performed in a public television special; *Paul Sorvino, An Evening of Song*. A deputy sheriff in Pennsylvania, Sorvino is legally able to carry a gun in different states. He is the father of Mira Sorvino, who won the Best Supporting Actress Oscar in Woody Allen's *Mighty Aphrodite*.

Paul Mercurio (b. 1963), aka Scott Hastings, the male lead in the 1992 film *Strictly Ballroom*, was originally asked to contribute choreography for the debut project of Australian director and friend Baz Luhrmann. Luhrmann was so impressed by Mercurio that he offered him the lead. Mercurio has since become film's version of a one-hit wonder.

Paul Muni – the American Award-winning and Tony Award-winning actor – is actually called Meshilem Meier Weisenfreud. He was born to a Jewish family in what is now the Scrabble-brilliant Lviv in the Ukraine. He starred in the original 1932 *Scarface* and was nominated for five Oscars, despite making only 25 films. In the fourth-season *M*A*S*H* episode Hawkeye Pierce describes his childhood in the 1930s and Muni's ubiquitous film appearances thus:

"You knew where you stood in those days. Roosevelt was always president, Joe Louis was always the champ, and Paul Muni played everybody."

PAUL ON THE SMALL SCREEN

Paul Michael Glaser, aka Hutch's partner Starsky, directed Arnold Schwarzenegger in *The Running Man* and played Captain Hook in pantomime at the Churchill Theatre, Bromley, Kent. At University, he was a room-mate of Andy Summers, the drummer in The Police. On *Starsky and Hutch*, Glaser commented: "We had a groundbreaking show with unique characters. But all people remember is the car."

Glaser lost his daughter Ariel and his first wife Elizabeth to AIDS. His wife contracted the disease after a blood transfusion during childbirth; she unknowingly passed the infection on to her daughter through breastfeeding. Glaser has one son, Jake, who is also HIV positive, contracted in the uterus. He is a fit, healthy young adult.

Paul Eddington is better known as Jim Hacker in the TV Comedy *Yes Minister* and Jerry Leadbetter in *The Good Life*. His acting career began in 1941 with the Entertainments National Service Association which, under the Ministry of Labour and National Service, is designed to provide entertainment to the HM Forces. Eddington, however, was asked to leave when it was discovered he was a pacifist and a conscientious objector, prompted by his Quaker principles. Shortly before his death, upon being asked what he wanted his epitaph to be, Eddington replied: "He did very little harm."

Paul Nicholas' father Oscar Beuselinck was an esteemed entertainment lawyer; his clients included The Rolling Stones, Richard Harris, Sean Connery and The Who.

On his official website **Paul Daniels** says his dislikes are: "Inefficiency, idleness, centre lane drivers, war, violence and murder, especially when they come in the name of religion, turning down charity and party invitations; but due to the amount of work it leaves little family time." Do you think that was in order?

He has the number plate, MAG 1C. On his "Did You Know" section it states: "Paul Daniels has entertained many millions of people from all walks of life both in this country and abroad. He continues to enthral audiences of all ages with a unique comedy style that never fails to impress, resulting in a truly magical and memorable experience for all."

The *Beverley Hillbillies* creator **Paul Henning** once met future President Harry S. Truman. Truman advised Henning to become a lawyer.

Paul Robinson, the character from Australian soap *Neighbours*, played by Stefan Dennis, appeared in the first episode in 1985 and was nicknamed Junior JR due to his resemblance to the *Dallas* character.

BBC TV programme *I'm With Stupid* featured disabled character **Paul** who befriends homeless Sheldon. Writer Danny Peak confirmed: "Paul, despite the fact that he's had a difficult life and has had a lot of challenges to face, is fairly devious and calculating and he's quite willing to take advantage of people." The idea came from Manchester writer Peter Keeley, who has cerebral palsy.

Paul Kaye, the alter ego of shock broadcaster journalist Dennis Pennis, graduated from Nottingham Trent University with a degree in theatre design. His Pennis style, accosting celebrities with questions ranging from the playful to the spiteful included asking Helena Christensen: "Why was the supermodel staring at the carton of orange juice... because it said concentrate." Asking Steve Martin: "How come you're not funny anymore?" Kaye later stated it was the sole interview/attack he regretted whilst playing the Pennis character.

To a puzzled Tom Hanks Pennis asked: "Did you enjoy playing Forrest last year? I don't know why they sold Collymore, you know?" His favourite film is Japanese anime offering *Princess Mononoke*, which he introduced on Film Four.

Actor **Paul Ruud**'s most famous role is Mike Hannigan, husband of *Friends'* Phoebe Buffay. Ruud is a self-confessed "mega-fan" of the TV show *Lost*. He says one of his long-held ambitions is to interview *Lost* star Emilie de Ravin, aka Claire.

Paul Robinson in Neighbours:

Paul: "Woah, you're a bit angry."
Toadie: "I'd have to calm down a lot to be a bit angry."

Big Brother II's Bubble, real name **Paul Ferguson**, was
voted out (of Channel Four's pass for sixth months of free
nightclub entry) amidst reports that the phone number
needed to register his eviction had been posted as a football
news service. Bubble and follow housemate Dean released
Standing Tall in the hope of becoming an unofficial World
Cup 2002 anthem.

Upon entering the house, **Paul Clarke**, from *Big Brother II*,
listed his pet hates as people who pick their nose in traffic,
tomatoes and classical opera. And they say British television
is being dumbed down.

POLITICAL PAULS

Born in Levin, New Zealand, **Sir Paul Beresford** is
Conservative MP for Mole Valley, Croydon. Beresford
was knighted, under Margaret Thatcher, for pioneering
the practice of hiring contractors to do council jobs and
services to inner city rehabilitation.

Paul Burstow, the Liberal Democrat MP for Sutton and
Cheam, prepared for life in Westminster by becoming a
buying assistant with Allied Shoe Repairs and working in
print sales with KallKwik Printers.

Paul Clark, Labour MP, was born in Gillingham and
represents his home town. Clark has an impressive average
of 75% attendance in divisions since 1997 and has, less
impressively, rebelled just seven times against the Labour
Government.

Paul Farrelly, Labour MP for Newcastle-under-Lyme was
deputy business editor of *The Independent on Sunday* before
joining *The Observer* in 1997 as the City Editor.

Paul Flynn, Labour MP for Newport West, had to pay
out more than £36,000 to settle a libel action brought
against him by Endowment Justice. Flynn criticised
the growing number of complaints against handlers of
endowment mortgages and actually named Endowment

Justice. Flynn paid their £35,450 legal costs, plus £1,000 in damages, which the company donated to the NSPCC.

The Labour MP **Paul Goggins** (b.1953), of Wythenshawe & Sale East fame, once claimed, on BBC Radio Five Live, that his family was the inspiration behind the Postman Pat character Mrs. Goggins. Goggins' uncle had known the books' author John Cunliffe. In 2006, in Parliament, he revealed that the people of Northern Ireland drink an average of 122 litres of carbonated drinks per year. This compares to the UK's 105 litres and Republic of Ireland's 109.

Despite having a largely unsuitable name for an MP, Wycombe's Conservative MP **Paul Goodman** is deputy editor of *The House Magazine*, which offers in-depth analysis of Parliament from inside the chamber.

Paul Holmes (b.1957), Liberal Democrat MP for Chesterfield, a history teacher for 22 years before taking over Tony Benn's seat, is an Honorary Associate of the National Secular Society. In March 2008, Holmes was, at the time of Fidel Castro's resignation, the only Liberal Democrat MP to sign an Early Day Motion praising the exiting Cuban leader. Holmes noted: "It is true Cuba has political prisoners and no free elections, but it has very good dentistry."

Hereford's Liberal Democrat **Paul Keetch** was once taken seriously ill while flying from Britain to the USA. Indeed, ninety minutes into the flight, the plane was turned around. The reason for Keetch's collapse has never been properly diagnosed. It is claimed, however, that his heart stopped for more than a minute and that he would have died had there not been a defibrillator on board.

Perhaps it was worrying about his constituency majority. At the 2005 General Election, Mr Keetch had a majority of just 962 (2.1%) over the Conservatives – the 589th smallest majority from 631 MPs. Keetch also founded the All Party Cider Group which creates (a wobbly) platform for the National Association of Cidermakers at Westminster.

The Rt. Hon Paul Murphy (b. 1948), Labour MP for the Welsh constituency of Torfaen and the Welsh Secretary of State, joined the Labour Party at 15. A practising Roman Catholic, in a free parliamentary vote in May 2008, Murphy voted for cutting the upper limit for abortions from 24 to 12 weeks, alongside fellow Cabinet ministers Ruth Kelly and Des Browne.

When Rochdale's Liberal Democrat MP **Paul Rowen** left secondary school he had three O levels. However, this didn't stop him becoming head of a secondary school. He cites U2's The Joshua Tree as his favourite piece of music. Incredibly, this did not impact his 2005 election to Parliament. Although it must have reduced his already wafer thin majority of just 442 seats – 606th from 631 MPs.

Pudsey's Labour MP **Paul Truswell** said his greatest achievement in Parliament was: "Helping obtain funding for local services including: five new primary schools under construction; extra resources for many other schools; 70 extra police officers and 50 extra community support officers… and the initial go-ahead for a Leeds Children's Hospital." Political commentator Byron Criddle's synopsis on Truswell's contribution was slightly less glowing: "conspicuous only for piloting through a bill to make off-licence staff liable for sales to under age customers." He also openly admits to enjoying U2.

Paul Boateng (b. 1951), the first black Cabinet minister when appointed as chief secretary to the treasury in 2002, likes to not focus on the colour of his skin. After his 2005 election, Boateng commented: "One of the major problems of an MP who is black is to be recognised simply as a Member of Parliament who is black rather than a black Member of Parliament; the idea that one is going into Parliament to represent black people is absolute baloney but one you constantly have to state is not the case."

Lord Swraj Paul is worth around £150m as the head of one of the biggest family-owned manufacturers in Britain. Now a Labour Peer, Paul came to Britain in 1965 to seek medical treatment for his two-year-old daughter who was dying of leukaemia. He stayed on in this country and gained British citizenship in 1976. He is no longer domiciled in the UK for tax purposes. He wrote Indira

Ghandi's biography. No-one answers his House of Lords phone when you call it.

Paul Weller's Into Tomorrow is the hold music when calling the Labour Party. Lyrics: "Round and round like a twisted wheel, spinning in attempt to find the feel. Find the path that will help us find a feeling of control over lives and minds."

British businessman **Paul Sykes** (b. 1943) is worth around £500m and has donated around £6m to Eurosceptic campaigns. He believes that the European Union is a forerunner to an undemocratic United States of Europe. He's come a long way. Born the son of a Barnsley miner, he left school with no qualifications and began his first business at 18; dismantling old buses and selling the engines to the Far East. A decade later he was building one of Britain's first out-of-town shopping centres – Sheffield's Meadowhall.

An aggressive debater who once described a political foe as "all tip and no iceberg", **Paul Keating** was the 24th Prime Minister of Australia. In 1992, a British tabloid dubbed him 'The Lizard of Oz' for placing his arm around Queen Elizabeth II. He has suggested that Sydney should be the capital of Australia, not Canberra, and collects French antique clocks.

Born on August 6th 1923 and a former Canadian defence minister, **Paul Hellyer** is clearly enjoying not having to toe the party line since leaving public office. Hellyer has publicly stated that: "To really fight this global warming thing, we're going to need the secret alien technologies that governments recovered from UFOs but have been hiding from us."

In November 2005, he told a University of Toronto audience: "The US military are preparing weapons which could be used against the aliens and could get us into an intergalactic war. The Bush Administration has finally agreed to let the military build a base on the moon, which will put them in a better position to keep track of the visitors from space and to shoot at them, if they so decide."

Justice for Paul?

An Australian family will sue the British Government after a coroner ruled their husband/father died due to a "serious failure" by Britain's military. RAF Flight-Lieutenant **Paul Pardoel** was Australia's first fatality in the Iraq War on January 30th 2005. His death could have been avoided if the Hercules C130k aircraft he was flying had been fitted with explosion suppressant foam (ESF), a safety device which prevents plane fuel tanks from exploding. All subsequent planes flying over Iraq and Afghanistan have since been fitted with ESF.

Paul the artist

Pablo Picasso's (b. 1881) full name is Pablo Diego José Francisco de Paula Juan Nepomuceno María de los Remedios Cipriano de la Santísima Trinidad Martyr Patricio Clito Ruíz y Picasso. While living in Paris during 1900, a destitute Picasso had to burn many of his paintings to stay warm. Rumour has it that Las Vegas casino magnate Steve Wynn, owner of Picasso's *Dream* painting, accidentally poked a hole through the £25m painting while showing his friends the portrait of Picasso's mistress Marie-Therese Walter.

SHOW ME THE MONET

Pablo Picasso is responsible for nine of the thirty most expensive paintings ever sold at auction.

Garçon à la pipe (6th most expensive) at	**$118.9**
Dora Maar au Chat (8)	**$101.8**
Les Noces de pierette (13)	**$85.7**
Yo, Picasso (16)	**$83.2**
Au Lapin Agile(22)	**$70.8**
Acrobate et jeune Arlequin (23)	**$70.2**
Femme aux Bras Croisés (24)	**$68.9**
Le Rêve (26)	**$65.0**
Femme assise dans un jardin (27)	**$64.2**

Paul Klee, he of fine lines, geometry and watercolours, produced nearly 10,000 works and was fascinated by childish art. The Nazi party deemed him "degenerate" and removed all his public exhibits. In 1933 he moved to Switzerland, was diagnosed with having scleroderma – a rare condition that hardens the skin – which affected his graphic style. Also a formidable musician, Klee played, for a time, violin with the Berne Symphony Orchestra. He is considered one of the masters of modern art. He once said: "A drawing is simply a line going for a walk."

French post-impressionist painter **Paul Cézanne** (b. 1839) was described by Picasso as: "My one and only master… Cezanne was like the father of us all." It is said that Cézanne formed the bridge between late 19th century impressionism and the early 20th century cubism. His interest lie in the simplification of naturally occurring forms to their geometric essentials and he wanted to "treat nature by the cylinder, the sphere, the cone". Cézanne's painting of a water jug and fruit bowls *Rideau, Cruchon et Compotier*, sold for $60.5 million, at the time of writing the seventeenth highest price paid at auction.

"The day is coming when a single carrot, freshly observed, will set off a revolution." **Paul Cezanne**

"When I judge art, I take my painting and put it next to a God-made object like a tree or flower. If it clashes, it is not art." **Paul Cezanne**

The commitment of British artist **Paul Nash** (b.1889) to his art was literally death-defying. Nash was an Official War Artist on World War I and II's frontline. At heart a surrealist, Nash's style was still incredibly lucid and evocative of the personal connection, emotion and philosophies of war. On his role as War Artist he wrote to his wife from The Front on 16th November 1917: "I am no longer an artist. I am a messenger who will bring back word from the men who are fighting to those who want the war to go on forever. Feeble, inarticulate will be my message, but it will have a bitter truth and may it burn their lousy souls."

Leading post-impressionist painter **Paul Gauguin** (b. 1848) spent time in the army and as a stockbroker in Denmark before committing to painting. He considered his work

Where Do We Come From? What Are We? Where Are We Going?
his best, it being one that contained the summation of his
ideas about life and his personal struggle with the meaning
of existence. Gauguin has been sainted by the Ecclesia
Gnostica Catholica, a modern revival of Gnosticism – the
movement that believes humans are divine souls trapped in
a material world created by an imperfect god.

Sculptor **Paul Howard Manship** (b. 1885) is most closely
associated with the golden statue 'Prometheus', which flies
across the base of the Rockefeller Center. However, he also
produced the inaugural John F. Kennedy medal.

Paul Signac was a French neo-impressionist painter
who helped develop the pointillist style. Pointillism is the
marked style of painting in which small distinct points of
primary colours create the impression of a wide selection of
secondary and intermediate colours.

"Only put off until tomorrow what you are willing to die
having left undone." **Pablo Picasso**

Nottingham's **Paul Sandby** was an English map maker
and landscape painter in watercolours, who, in 1768, was
one of the founders of The Royal Academy. In 1746 – as
part of Lieutenant-Colonel David Watson's plans to make
the Scottish clans English subjects – following the Jacobite
rising of 1745, Sandby mapped the remote Scottish
Highlands. The survey was produced at a scale of 1 inch to

1000 yards and became the first incarnation of the modern Ordnance Survey map.

PAUL – GOING FOR A SONG

Paul Weller, aka The Modfather, declined a CBE in the Queen's Birthday Honours list of 2006. In 1983, The Jam broke The Beatles' record of seven singles in the Top 100 at the same time; Polydor re-released their entire back catalogue following the band split and 14 singles placed in the same week. In 2002, when Virgin Radio compiled their top 100 British artists of all time, Weller came in at number 21; The Style Council were number 97, and The Jam fifth.

The song that more or less launched Weller, Going Underground, was reportedly supposed to be a double A side with Dreams of Children. A mistake by a French Press plant gave Going Underground 'A' status providing the springboard for the song and Weller's lengthy success.

Scottish singer **Paolo Nutini** was an ambassador for Puma in 2008. On the advert, he performs his track 'New Shoes'. What would The Sex Pistols have made of it?

Musician **Paul Simon** is left-handed but he plays his guitar with his right. He was once married to Carrie Fisher, aka Princess Leia, for just shy of a year between August 1983 and July 1984. Named *Tom & Jerry* by their record company, it was under this name that the duo of Simon and Art Garfunkel had their early success.

Today he's a member of the US Rock and Roll Hall of Fame, and, in 2006, was described by *Time* magazine as one of "The 100 people who shape our world". Paul Simon is the only artist to have had *The Muppet Show* use his songs exclusively for a single episode.

"Why am I so soft in the middle when the rest of my life is so hard." **Paul Simon**

"Improvisation is too good to leave to chance." **Paul Simon** in *International Herald Tribune*

Paul Jabara, who won the 1978 Oscar for best original song *Last Dance* from *Thank God It's Friday*, was the creator of the AIDS movement red ribbon. He also wrote *It's Raining Men* with Paul Shaffer, the bald musician sidekick of David Letterman.

In 2007 **Paul Potts** (b. 1970) went from a shy, retiring, ill-dentisted, Carphone Warehouse manager to a British tenor sensation thanks to the winning of ITV's *Britain's Got Talent*. Controversy surrounded the merits of Potts' amateur status. While portrayed as a mobile phone salesman by the show, he had, in fact, already appeared in a concert for the Royal Philharmonic Orchestra. His album *One Chance* was number one in 14 different countries for a total of 56 weeks. Potts met his wife Julie-Ann in an internet chat room. And he's had his teeth done.

Australian rugby league giant **Paul 'The Chief' Harragon** (b. 1968) weighs 111 kg and stands at 193cm tall. On Saturday 1 September 2007, his single That's Gold, a parody of Spandau Ballet's 1980s hit Gold, debuted at number two on the Australia Record Industry Association Singles Chart.

Paul Reed Smith (b. 1956) is one of the world's leading luthiers (guitar maker, from the French word luth from lute) and the founder and owner of PRS Guitars. Smith would often take his guitars backstage at concerts, and got his break when Derek St. Holmes, of the Ted Nugent Band, agreed to try out the second guitar Smith had ever made. St. Holmes eventually sold the instrument for $200, not realising how big Paul Reed Smith was going to get.

Guitarist **Paul Gilbert**, considered one of the fastest guitarists in the world, teaches at Hollywood's Guitar Institute of Technology. Yes, there is one.

An original member, and lead singer, of The Housemartins (alongside Quentin Cook, aka Norman Cook, aka Fat Boy Slim) and The Beautiful South, **Paul Heaton** disbanded the latter group in January 2007 citing "musical similarities". During his time with The Beautiful South, all money was split equally between all members of the band.

Paul, of 1960s folk revival group Peter, Paul and Mary fame, is actually called **Noel (Paul) Stookey**. Stookey's best-known solo composition is the 1971 ditty: The Wedding

Song (There is Love). He wrote the song as a wedding gift for fellow American singer Peter Yarrow, and refused to perform it publicly until Yarrow requested it at a concert where his wife was present. Stookey subsequently relinquished copyright of the song, bequeathing it instead to the Public Domain Foundation. Yarrow had previously written Peter, Paul and Mary's most famous song Puff the Magic Dragon.

"I've lived a life that's full, I've travelled each and ev'ry highway. And more, much more than this, I did it my way"
Paul Anka in *My Way*

Born December 17th 1949, former lead singer of Free, **Paul Rodgers**, is from Middlesbrough. He didn't let that hamper him. The band's All Right Now was number one in twenty countries and has been played more than 2,000,000 times on UK radio. Paul's second wife Cynthia Kereluk – a TV fitness celebrity in her native country – is a former Miss Canada and entered the 1984 Miss Universe competition.

Paul Carrack was a member of Ace, Squeeze, Mike & The Mechanics and Roxy Music. He played keyboards on The Smiths' eponymous debut album, Elton John's Something About The Way You Look Tonight and Candle In The Wind '97.

He might look foolish and be somewhat glib, but **Paul Shaffer**, the *David Letterman Show* sidekick, is a well-respected musical director. He was musical director for the We Are the World finale of Live-Aid in 1985; *The Blues Brothers'* (John Belushi and Dan Aykroyd) double platinum album and national tour; closing concert at the 1996 Olympic Games; and the 1999 Concert of the Century at the White House which included Eric Clapton, B.B. King and Gloria Estefan.

Paul Young, the voice of Wherever I Lay My Hat (That's My Home) was also the voice of the Streetband's 1978 novelty track Toast. He performed the opening vocals on the 1984 Band Aid single Do They Know It's Christmas?. Young's biggest worldwide hit, the 1985 Everytime You Go Away reached number one on the US pop charts. It was actually a cover version of a track on Hall & Oates 1980 album, Voices.

One of the world's leading dance and electronica DJs, **Paul Van Dyk** grew up in East Berlin where he kept in touch with the world beyond the Berlin Wall by secretly listening to the popular, but forbidden, Western radio stations RIAS (Radio in the American Sector) and mix tapes occasionally smuggled into the country and copied among school friends. In 2005 and 2006, *DJ Magazine* named him the best DJ in the world. He has not been out of the top five since 2000.

Paul Oakenfold was named *DJ Magazine*'s top DJ in the world in 1999. As a 21-year-old, in New York, his fake ID earned entry to superclub Studio 54 where he pretended to be a journalist from *NME* and interviewed Bob Marley. Back in the UK, he signed DJ Jazzy Jeff and The Fresh Prince (aka Will Smith). He became a British promoter and agent for the Beastie Boys and Run DMC and has worked on the film scores on *Big Brother*, *The Bourne Identity*, *The Matrix Loaded* and *Pirates of the Caribbean*. He's a fully qualified chef and would like to work with Eminem and Limp Biskit.

Paul King, he of Love & Pride and VH1 fame, graduated from Coventry Drama School and considered joining the West Midlands Police before opting for his first band, rock-ska outfit, The Reluctant Stereotypes.

THE INEVITABLE MCCARTNEY SECTION

Paul McCartney (b. June 18th 1942), real name James Paul McCartney, is listed in the *Guinness Book of Records* as the most successful musician and composer in popular music history. He has 60 gold discs and sales of over 100 million singles. At 3,700, *Yesterday* is listed as the most covered song in history. It has been played more than seven million times on American television and radio.

McCartney is one of Britain's wealthiest men. On deciding the divorce settlement with Heather Mills, Justice Bennett estimated his wealth at around £400 million. McCartney's company MPL Communications owns the copyrights to more than 3,000 songs, including Buddy Holly's back catalogue and the musicals *Guys and Dolls*, *A Chorus Line* and *Grease*.

"It was Elvis who really got me hooked on beat music. When I heard Heartbreak Hotel I thought, this is it!"
Paul McCartney

Paul McCartney wrote music before lyrics. While he was composing the song Yesterday he used the words "scrambled eggs" so he could see what would fit into the rest of the song. He wrote Hey Jude for John Lennon's son, Julian, who was upset by his parents' divorce, in the car on his way to cheer him up.

Paul McCartney paid Heather Mills a £24.3m divorce settlement and while it was a drop in the ocean it is interesting that Mr. Justice Bennett said "there is absolutely no evidence" to support Mills' estimation of McCartney's wealth at £800m. The judge approximated £400m.

Paul McCartney's Lucy In The Sky With Diamonds actually wasn't meant to say LSD. It was a drawing that John Lennon's son Julian brought home from school. Lucy was a kid in his school.

Paul Is Dead is the delicious urban myth that former Beatle Paul McCartney died in 1966 and was replaced by a look-alike and sound-alike. The most common tale is that on Wednesday 9th November 1966, at 5am, McCartney, while working on the Sgt. Pepper's Lonely Hearts Club Band album, stormed out of a recording session after an argument and crashed his Austin-Healey. Proof?

Look at the lyrics in Beatles songs, for example A Day In The Life's "He didn't notice that the lights had changed"; She's Leaving Home's "Wednesday morning at 5 o'clock as the day begins"; and Lady Madonna's "Wednesday morning papers didn't come". While visually, the fact that McCartney is the only barefooted Beatle, and out of step, on the cover of Abbey Road. Watertight, no?

Paul McCartney plays the guitar left-handed. The guitar on which he learned his first chords sold for £330,000 at a July 2006 auction at London's Abbey Road Studios.

BACK TO THE OTHERS...

Better known by his nickname Guigsy, former Oasis
bass player **Paul McGuigan** (b. 1971) wrote, alongside
journalist Paolo Hewitt, a book about Reading Football
Club's errant genius Robin Friday; *The Greatest Footballer You
Never Saw*. Oasis lead singer Noel Gallagher said that over
the course of their 17-year relationship he had had around
one hour's cumulative conversation with McGuigan.

The song Paul, also known as **Paul der Bademeister** (Paul
the pool attendant) was the first single from German band
Die Arzte. Paul is about a confident swimming pool attendant
and includes the lyrics: "Paul, Paul, Paul, Paul, Paul is mad!
Paul is a lifeguard in the swimming pool on the corner. Girls
come from far and wide, they love his chest, he watches over
them with his small gold chain, which brings him luck. Paul is
an only child, and likes nice girls, who he throws off the 10-
metre board (ha!). He flies like Superman. We will gladly pay
our admission fee because Paul is a most beautiful lifeguard
in the whole world." Only in Germany, and bless them for it.

Paul Hewson (b. 1960), more commonly known at Bono,
is the only person to be nominated for an Academy Award,
Golden Globe, Grammy, Nobel Peace Prize and a knighthood!
Bono's mother died in 1974 after suffering a cerebral aneurysm
at her father's funeral. Bono was 14. Rumour has it that he was
nicknamed *Bono Vox* by friend Gavin Friday. Bono originally
disliked the name, but upon learning it loosely translated to
"good voice", went along with it.

On his constant wearing of sunglasses he told *Rolling Stone* magazine: "I have very sensitive eyes to light. If somebody takes my photograph, I will see the flash for the rest of the day. My right eye swells up. I've a blockage there, so that my eyes go red a lot. So it's part vanity, it's part privacy and part sensitivity."

Bono is a mononymous person: someone who is known by an individual name determined by custom or culture. For example: Voltaire, Eminem or Pele.

Gary Glitter's real name is **Paul Francis Gadd**. He had 26 hit singles and spent 180 weeks in the UK top 100 music charts before claiming notoriety as a child sex offender. In 1997 child pornography images were discovered by the Bristol Cribbs Causeway branch of PC World.

Les Paul (b. 1915), the pioneer of the solid-body electric guitar, was actually born Lester Polfuss on June 9th 1915. His first creation, The Log was a length of common fence post with bridge, guitar neck, and pickup attached. Paul took his design to Gibson who loved it and it became today's Les Paul. In 1961, however, Gibson changed the design slightly without Paul's knowledge. He first saw the 'new' Gibson Les Paul in a music shop window, and disliked it. Though his contract required him to pose with the guitar, he asked Gibson to remove his name from the headstock – it became the Gibson SG. Early in his career, Bing Crosby sponsored Paul's recording experiments. He is the godfather of rock guitarist Steve Miller of the Steve Miller Band.

Kevin Jonas, the only non-teen member of Disney's hard-rocking celebrity virgins the Jonas Brothers, is really called **Paul Kevin Jonas II**. Jonas shot to stardom with the aptly titled Disney film, *Camp Rock*.

Kiss guitarist **Paul Stanley** is actually called Stanley Harvey Eisen. Stanley's Kiss persona is 'The Starchild'. He often dresses as *Star Wars* character Darth Maul and refers to himself as Maul Stanley.

Best known as rock guitarist with the band Free, **Paul Kossoff** died in 1976 from a drug-induced heart attack while on a plane flight from Los Angeles to New York at the age of just 25. Sky high, man.

Paul Williams was one of the founding members and original lead singer of The Temptations and is most closely associated with For Once In My Life. His tumultuous life ended in a 1973 suicide. According to the coroner, Williams had used his right hand to shoot himself in the left side of his head. In addition, the gun used in the shooting was found to have fired two shots, only one of which had killed Williams.

TEN GREAT FILM CHARACTERS NAMED PAUL

Paul Sheldon (James Caan – *Misery*)
Best-selling novelist Sheldon is returning home from
completing his most recent book at a Colorado hideaway
when a freak blizzard causes him to crash. He is 'rescued'
by uber-fan Annie Wilkes who proceeds to kidnap, drug and
cripple her helpless charge.

Paul Varjak (George Peppard – *Breakfast at Tiffany's*)
Struggling writer Paul Varjak moves into a New York
apartment block and, understandably, becomes enamoured
by Holly Golightly, played by Audrey Hepburn. In public
she's flirty, sophisticated and confident; in private she's
nervy and self-obsessed.

Paul Kersey (Charles Bronson – *Death Wish*)
Liberal architect has his world torn apart when his wife is
murdered and his daughter raped. Paul goes to Arizona on
compassionate leave and is given a gun. He returns to New
York a vigilante with revenge against anyone committing
crime on his mind.

Paul 'Wrecking' Crewe (Burt Reynolds/Adam Sandler –
The Longest Yard)
Made in 1974 and re-made in 2005, Crewe is a football
player-turned-convict who organises an inmates versus prison
guards game. He is asked to throw the contest in return for
early release but doesn't want to betray his fellow prisoners.

Paul Cicero (**Paul Sorvino** – *Goodfellas*)
Based on real-life mobster Paul Vario, Cicero is a local mob boss. Cicero and his associate Jimmy Conway help cultivate the developing criminal career of Henry Hill.

Paul Vitti (Robert De Niro – *Analyze This/Analyze That*)
When mobster Vitti suffers a crisis of confidence, threatening his ability to lead his criminal empire, he turns to professional help from Dr Ben Sobel. The FBI approaches Sobel with an offer he can't refuse: betray Vitti by wearing a wire or spend a long time in a federal prison.

Paul Rivers (Sean Penn – *21 Grams*)
Amid three separate stories, three characters are tied together by a hit and run. Jack kills Cristina's husband and children with his truck in a hit-and-run accident, killing them. Christina's husband's heart is donated to Paul, who begins his recovery.

Comte Paul de Raymond (Alfred Molina – *Chocolat*)
When a single mother and her six-year-old daughter move to rural France and open a chocolate shop – across the street from the local church – and decide to trade on Sundays they are met by the sceptical Comte Paul de Raymond.

Paul Sunday (**Paul Dano** – *There Will Be Blood*)
Daniel Plainview is an oil man. When Paul Sunday asks

Plainview to dig for oil at his family home, he can't resist. However, Paul's brother Eli sees the opportunity to mine some of Plainview's wealth for his unorthodox church.

Dr Paul Carruthers (Bela Lugosi – *The Devil Bat*)
Bela Lugosi is, to his neighbours, a kindly doctor and research scientist. However, in his top secret laboratory, Carruthers is conducting a personal experiment to create an oriental shaving lotion AND a giant bat who hates the smell of the lotion. They don't make 'em like they used to.

OLYMPIC PAULS

Upon his return from Beijing 2008, **Paul Manning**, Britain's world-record breaking gold medal cyclist, told the *Daily Mirror* newspaper that after retiring from cycling at 33, he did not have a job. The former newspaper boy and shelf stacker confirmed: "Now the excitement is dying down it's hit me that I'm going to have to get back in Civvy Street and motivate myself instead of going out on a bike ride and enjoying that." The team pursuit specialist had spent six hours a day for the last twenty years on his bike. Manning had enjoyed £25,000 a year lottery funding.

Upon his return from the Beijing Olympics, **Paul Goodison**, gold medal winner in the men's Laser sailing class, wore his gong to the Sheffield United game against Cardiff City. The game ended 0-0.

Denmark's sailing God **Paul Elvstrøm** is one of only three Olympians to win the same individual event four times in a row. He is also one of only four athletes to compete in eight or more Olympics from 1948 to 1988. Elvstrøm was also a real innovator. One of his most successful inventions is a device set into the underwater section of the boat's hull that can be lowered to remove water from the cockpit by means of the suction generated by the water flow.

Born in 1886, Welsh swimmer **Paulo Radmilovic** won four Olympic titles in a 22-year Olympic career. He earned his first Amateur Swimming Association title when victorious in the open water five mile race in the River Thames in 1907.

Radmilovic won four gold medals – three in water polo, London 1908, Stockholm 1912 and Antwerp 1920 and one in swimming, London 1908 – across three successive Olympic Games. It was a British record until Sir Steve Redgrave came along. Radmilovic, who had a Croatian father and Irish mother, was one of the original ten inducted into the Welsh Sports Hall of Fame in 1988. His medals, however, have never been found.

Kenyan **Paul Tergat** held the world marathon record from 2003 until 2007 covering the 26.22 mile race in 2 hours, 4 minutes and 55secs – which is an average of 12.59mph. Ironically, his record was set on September 28th 2003 in the Berlin Marathon, exactly five years to the day that Haile Gebrselassie set the new record of 2 hours, 3 minutes and 59 seconds. The race is based on the legend of Pheidippides and his 21.4 mile run from Marathon to Athens to announce the Greek's victory in the Battle of Marathon. The current distance of 26.22 miles has been in effect since 1924.

Born in 1874, Frenchman **Paul Masson** won three of the six cycling events – 1km time trial, 10km track race and 1,000m sprint – at the inaugural 1896 Olympics. After the Athens Games, he turned professional and changed his name to **Paul Nossam**, to differentiate himself from the wine maker. He was placed third in the world professional sprint championship in 1897.

Five-time Olympic fencing medallist **Paul Anspach** is a legend in his native Belgium, where he is revered for his gold and silver medal-winning exploits in the London (1908), Stockholm (1912), Antwerp (1920) and Paris (1924) Olympics. He was a major contributor to the formation of the Belgian Olympic Committee in 1906, and served as the president of the International Fencing Association from 1933 to 1948. During World War II, the Association's activity was suspended when the German Gestapo removed its files. They have never been recovered.

PAULS FROM THE TOYBOX

Paul is a roaming *Pokémon* trainer. Paul is a stern,
excessively demanding trainer whose only concern for
Pokémon is of their ability to act in battle. As such, Paul
always checks his newly captured *Pokémon* with his Pokédex
to learn what attacks they know. He strongly dislikes weak
Pokémon and has a habit of releasing them if they do not
meet up to his high expectations. He believes that forming a
bond with his fighters only dilutes a *Pokémon*'s true potential
and turns them into slackers.

Paul Phoenix is one of only four fighters to appear in
all nine incarnations of the *Tekken* video game series – the
others being Heihachi Mishima, Yoshimitsu and Nina
Williams. Paul's signature move is the Deathfist, a mid-
hitting straight punch which deals huge damage, and
knocks his opponent flying. In the *Tekken* story arc, Paul
is a karate/judo expert who always seems to lose due to
some unforeseen complication – a traffic jam, fatigue,
underestimating his opponent, partying the night before a
fight. Cool.

KNOCKOUT PAULS

Former IBF World Lightweight boxing champion **Paul 'The Pittsburgh Kid' Spadafora** has had every single one of his 42 undefeated professional bouts watched by his grandfather. He almost didn't make it to pro boxing; in the early 1990s he was shot in the ankle by a policeman while travelling in a friend's car. In 2003, despite a glittering boxing career, Spadafora was arrested and accused of shooting his girlfriend. In 2005, Spadafora began 32 months in jail for the crime. In between, on $50,000 bail, he had been arrested for crashing into a car while drunk and attempted suicide. After serving his jail sentence, on April 25th 2008 he impressively returned to the ring, out-pointing Shad Howard 80-72.

Paul 'The Punisher' Williams, the WBO Welterweight World Champion, started boxing after a school bus driver saw him fighting on his way home. The driver took him to the South Carolina Aiken Boxing Club.

Paul 'The Magic Man' Malignaggi (b. 1980), former IBF junior welterweight champion, was born in Brooklyn, New York and then moved to Syracuse, Italy. Malignaggi, thanks to his excellent hand speed, utilises the Thomas Hearns stance (left arm kept beside his waist, right hand at the chest level, leaving his head completely exposed, punching from his hips). He has modelled in *Esquire* and *Playboy* and is fluent in Italian and Spanish.

Paul Pender (1930-2003), the former Middleweight Boxing Champion of the World, was the first man to beat Sugar Ray Robinson twice. In the first fight against Robinson, as a massive underdog, Pender placed a bet of $2,000 on himself to win; he was going to join the police force if he had lost. Pender was a real tough nut. In a fight against Gene Fullmer on February 14th 1955, on the way to a points defeat, he broke his left hand in round four and his right hand in round six!

PAUL, A MAN WHO KNITS AMERICAN FOLKLORE AND HISTORY TOGETHER LIKE A BIG FOLKY SCARF

Paul Bunyan was created from the imagination of journalist James MacGillivray in or around 1906 and is a famous American myth. A lumberjack who appears in tall tales of US folklore, Bunyan is a gargantuan man who, when he was born, it took five storks to carry. When he was old enough to clap and laugh, the vibrations broke every window in the house.

Paul and his pet blue ox 'Babe' dug the Grand Canyon. Huge wooden statues of the man-giant litter Michigan, Wisconsin and Minnesota including the world's largest wood carving at Sequoia National Park. Akeley is birthplace and home of the world's largest Paul Bunyan Statue and the kneeling Paul Bunyan is 20 feet tall. He might be the claimed 33 feet tall, if he were standing.

Paul Revere has a very special place in American history, and has, indeed, become a synonym for healthy rebellion. Revere played his part in the American War of Independence success thanks to his 'midnight ride', made on April 18th 1775 between Boston and Lexington.

Revere borrowed a horse – reportedly a Narragansett Pacer named Brown Betty, a small chestnut mare – and rode from Boston to Lexington yelling, "The British are coming". As a result of Revere's 'warning' ride, the Lexington minutemen were ready the next morning for the British, and for the historic Battle of Lexington that would mark the beginning of the American Revolution.

Depending on where you sit, **Corporal Paul Weinert** was hero or villain in the 1890 Battle of Wounded Knee, (since re-christened The Massacre at Wounded Knee) the last major battle between the Sioux Indians and the US. At the time, many Sioux sought deliverance in a new mysticism called Wovoka; they believed their 'Ghost Shirts' would protect them from bullets. Weinert, who won a Medal of Honour for his actions at the helm of a Hotchkiss Mountain Howitzer, fired two-pound shells on the Indians that exploded upon impact, spraying deadly shrapnel in all directions.

In the early morning of August 6th 1945, **Colonel Paul Tibbets**, as pilot of the B-29 'Enola Gay' – named after his mother – flew into the history books. Just four hours into the flight, Tibbets told his crew that they carried the world's first atomic bomb and were going to drop it on Hiroshima, a city of 350,000 located in the south-west of Japan's largest island, Honshu. At 8.16am the bomb was released and detonated a few thousand feet above ground. The bomb, nicknamed 'Little Boy' is estimated to have killed or wounded 130,000 people.

Multi-lingual American actor, athlete, Basso cantante concert singer, writer and civil rights activist, **Paul Robeson** was a special man. When winning an academic scholarship to Rutgers University as a 17-year-old he was the only black student on campus. He excelled at American football, baseball, basketball and track and field. Throughout his life, Robeson fought against repression and was one of the first black men to play serious roles in the primarily white American theatre.

He played Joe in the 1928 London production of *Showboat* and sang the definitive Ol' Man River. During the 1940s, his black nationalist and anti-colonialist activities brought him to the attention of Senator Joseph McCarthy. Despite his contributions as an entertainer to the Allied Forces during World War II, Robeson was singled out as a major threat to American democracy and in 1950 his passport was revoked meaning he could no longer travel abroad to perform. However, his international appeal is such that, in 1983, the East German government honoured him with a postage stamp. He spoke fifteen languages.

RECORD-BREAKING PAULS

Paul D. Camp Community College in Franklin, Virginia set the record for the world's longest paper chain on June 4th and 5th 2005. It measured an incredible 54.33 miles.

St. Paul Minnesota can claim to be the home of the largest banana split ever made. It measured one mile in length and contained 33,000 scoops of ice cream and over 10,000 bananas.

<hr>

HE DOES WHAT?!

Connecticut native **Dr. Paul Aho** is an international agribusiness economist who specialises in projects related to the poultry industry. Aho operates his own consulting company called 'Poultry Perspective'. Surely it should have been Chickening Out?

<hr>

"Work is a necessity for man. Man invented the alarm clock"
Pablo Picasso

HE DID WHAT?!

Paul Barth, the Mayor of Louisville, Kentucky from 1905 to 1907, purchased an expensive saddle horse with city funds, justifying it as transportation for his duties as mayor. The press reported on the scandal so viciously that Barth eventually shot himself with a revolver in his office lavatory. However, over 30,000 people reportedly attended his funeral.

A 71-year-old Brit laboured three years to make a four foot high replica of **St. Paul's Cathedral** out of fruitcake. Oh, the irony.

When an estimated twelve cities sat glued to Public Television to watch the live broadcast of Philadelphia doctors reconstructing the skull of fifteen-month-old Michele Miller, her parents were equally absorbed. The girl's parents Lynn and **Paul Miller** watched *The Wizard of Oz* on another channel.

In 2006, gospel preacher **Paul Wren** of Carbonville, Illinois wanted to prove and demonstrate the strength of God's love. What better to do than to offer to lift the heaviest man in his congregation with his bare teeth? Step forward Joe Pearce, who weighed well over 18 stone.

With Pearce buckled into a harness, Wren placed the leather strap between his teeth and began to pull and strain and grunt until the pressure ripped five front teeth from his mouth. He regained composure enough to complete the thirty-minute sermon. However, many parishioners reputedly left to save laughing at his God-given lisp.

Newspapers usually decline to name the victims of sex crimes. However, perhaps this victim of a Russian Orthodox priest in Alaska should have shown a little bit of self-censure: **Paul Sidebottom** was happy for his name to be published.

A GOOD WALK SPOILED?

When Jean Van de Velde famously threw away a three-shot
lead on the final holes of golf's 1999 Open at Carnoustie,
Scottish golfer **Paul Lawrie** was the man to benefit.
At no time during the Open's 72 holes had Lawrie led
the competition. He moved level with Van de Velde and
American Justin Leonard after the Frenchman's collapse
and went on to win the competition on the four-hole play-
off. Also, Lawrie came back from the largest deficit in Open
history; he was ten shots behind Van de Velde going into the
final day.

Irish golfer **Paul McGinley** may be most famous for
holing the winning putt at Ireland's K Club in the 2002
Ryder Cup, but his finest moment arguably came when
offering a handshake to JJ Henry earlier in the same
competition. As Henry lined up a long, pressure putt to
halve their match, McGinley, seeing a streaker had run
across Henry's field of vision promptly offered his hand and
shook on the draw. It was a gesture which meant Henry
didn't have to take the putt and the hole would be halved.

Golfer **Paul Casey** managed to offend around 250 million
people in November 2004 when he gave a tongue-in-cheek
interview to *The Sunday Times*. On the US Ryder Cup team
he noted: "Oh, we properly hate them. We wanted to beat
them as badly as possible" and added that he thought
Americans were "insular". The remarks sparked outrage
in the USA, despite the fact that Casey has an American

wife and coach. Casey had to apologise for saying he "hated" Americans after receiving a flood of e-mails which prevented him from sleeping.

The richest Pauls in Britain according to *The 2008 Times Rich List*

47= **Lord Paul** and family £1,500m – Industry
146= **Paul Sykes** £550m – Property
158= **Sir Paul McCartney** £500m – Music, Inheritance
251= **Paul Ruddock** £350m – Finance
292= **Paul Marshall** £280m – Finance
312= **Sir Paul Smith** £260m – Fashion
344= **Paul Newey** £240m – Finance
366= **Paul Caddick** and family £220m – Construction
453= **Paul Kemsley** £180m – Property
453= **Paul Thwaites** £180m – Property
480= **Paul Day and family** £172m – Haulage
644= **Paul Gregg and family** £120m – Leisure
701= **Paul Stoddart** £115m – Transport
724= **Paul Deighton** £110m – Finance
746= **Paul Gower** £109m – Computer games
780= **Paul Leach and family** £102m – Property
784= **Paul Rooney** £100m – Estate agency
784= **Paul Roy** £100m – Finance
879= **Paul Dunkley** £90m – Car sales
915= **Paul Harrison** £87m – Construction
1116= **Paul Upward** £71m – Property
1118= **Paul Smith and family** £70m – Estate agency
1178= **Paul Gibbons** £69m – Media, Golf
1197= **Paul Bassi** £65m – Property
1246= **Paul Rowley** £62m – Construction
1259= **Paul Green** £60m – Property
1259= **Paul Hodgkinson** £60m – Construction
1331= **Paul Wells and family** £58m – Food
1355= **Paul Hunt and family** £55m – Food

1355= **Paul Rider** £55m – Construction
1415= **Paul Rackham and family** £52m – Property
1446= **Paul Barry-Walsh** £50m – Internet
1446= **Paul Williams** £50m Property
1621= **Paul Anderson** £45m – Publishing
1794= **Paul Beck** £40m – Business services
1794= **Paul Brewer** £40m – Finance
1794= **Paul Firmin and family** £40m – Transport
1794= **Paul Fletcher and family** £40m – Food
1794= **Paul Goldstein** £40m – Ski clothing

American rap artist **Paul Beauregard**, aka **DJ Paul**, won the 2006 Oscar for original song It's Hard Out Here For A Pimp. The first verse's lyrics include the lines: "In my eyes I done seen some crazy thangs in the streets/Gotta couple hoes workin' on the changes for me/But I gotta keep my game tight like Kobe on game night/Like takin' from a ho don't know no better, I know that ain't right."

You decide.

ST. PAUL, MINNESOTA. THE CITY YOU HAVE TO VISIT

Russell Daniel Angus, complaining of chronic pain,
wanted to have his testicles removed. When conventional
medical staff refused to do the job, he hired other **St. Paul**
professionals to take off his testicles. When police were
called by his daughter, they found a makeshift operating
room set up in the upper level of the house, bright lights,
an operating table, medical supplies and equipment, and a
camera. Angus was still bleeding, and there was blood in the
living room, hall and bathroom.

In 2006, Randy Bailey of **St. Paul, Minnesota**, decided
to dash down the street to his local Burger King to grab
a 'Whopper'. However, he was under house arrest with
an ankle monitor that goes off after four minutes. Bailey
was determined to get back before the alarm went off
but slow service sent him into a frenzy and he caused
over $1,000 worth of damage to the drive-thru window
before going home. Police visited Bailey's home to arrest
the man. Not for breaking the curfew, but for criminal
damage. Bailey had made it back home in time with
seconds to spare.

Bank tellers at **St. Paul Credit Union** told the city council
about an employee of the parking meter department when
he kept depositing hundreds of dollars in coins into his
account.

Police in **St. Paul** raided the home of bookmaker Max Weisberg in February 1999 and impounded $127,000 bringing the total seized from him over the last decade to over $600,000. Weisberg, 75, was not prosecuted. Despite being a genius with numbers Weisberg has a reported IQ of just 80 and, prosecutors believe, that he cannot comprehend why gambling should be illegal.

⟫━◆━⟪

PAUL, MEET PAULA

"God created man and, finding him not sufficiently alone, gave him a companion to make him feel his solitude more keenly." **Paul Valéry**

UNLUCKY PAULS

In March 2007, BA first-class passenger **Paul Trinder** – flying from Delhi to London at a cost of over £3,000 – thought he had a vacant seat next to him for the nine-hour flight. However, a lady died in economy and became Trinder's seat mate all the way home.

Austrian scientist **Paul Kammerer** wanted to prove the existence of Lamarckianism, the theory that says acquired characteristics can be passed to one's offspring within a single generation. Put more plainly; you get hurt in an accident, get a limp, your kids are born with a limp… Most toads mate in water, Midwife Toads mate on land. Most toads have black, scaly bumps on their hind limbs to help them hang onto each other while mating, Midwife Toads don't.

Kammerer filled fish tanks full of water, placed Midwife Toads in and waited as generations of toads were born and died. Black bumps appeared; scientific community astounded. Until, Dr Noble, Curator of Reptiles at the American Museum of Natural History, found not black, scaly marks on hind limbs but subcutaneous ink spots. Someone had injected black ink beneath the surface of the Midwife's Toads skin. Kammerer humiliated. Must have been one of his assistants, he said.

In 2000, the Nebraska Bar Association denied the application of **Paul Converse** concluding, based on his law school record, that he is too obnoxious, disruptive, abusive, intemperate and irresponsible even to be a lawyer.

In November 2007, **Dr Paul A. Schum**, the 50-year-old head teacher at Bethlehem Catholic High School in Kentucky, USA was arrested by Louisville police dressed as a woman in bondage gear. Officer Phil Russell confirmed: "He was wearing an all-black, leather, woman's outfit, fishnet stockings and women's black plastic breasts." He won out against a charge of prostitution but lost his job.

The Select Board of Springfield, Vermont denied **Paul Murphy**'s application for a liquor license, but based the decision on his largely incomprehensible paperwork, not because he wanted to sell alcohol from his cell at Massachusetts State prison.

In August 1987, the owner of a wool mill in Thompson, Connecticut, **Paul G. Thomas**, 47, was operating a pinwheel dressing machine when an accident struck. The contraption rolls wool yarn from a large spool to smaller ones and as Mr. Thompson reached in to make a minor adjustment on the machine he lost balance and fell forward onto one of the smaller, fast spinning spools. While hugging the spool, Thomas – in less than an estimated three minutes – first became bound then completely covered with 800 yards of yarn, causing him to suffocate and die.

Nixon's list of complete political opponents had five Pauls on it. American real estate developer and philanthropist **Paul Milstein**; President of the International Union Electrical, Radio & Machine Workers **Paul Jennings**; innovative economic thinker **Paul Samuelson**; actor **Paul Newman** and US Diplomat, who served under Nixon, **Paul Warnke**. The master list of Nixon political opponents was compiled to supplement the original 20-strong Enemies List initially considered opponents of Nixon.

Paul Winter, 42, came up snake eyes when, in 2008, he was shot dead by the ex-husband of a woman he married after meeting on a gambling website. Winter was killed in front of his new wife and her seven-year-old twins by Cristobal Palacio, Jennifer Winter's former husband.

Winter moved from Tunbridge Wells to Miami in 2006 to marry Jennifer. The couple had been dropping Mrs Winter's twins off at her ex-husband's after school when the shooting happened. It is alleged that Palacio emerged from his house and began yelling, before shooting Mr Winter, a graphic designer, six times in the chest.

In May 2007, artist **Paul Messenger** was fuming after his exhibit was mistakenly thrown away. Messenger's work, 36,000 feet of red tape was titled: "The Depravity of Society Juxtaposed Against the Apathy of Contemporary Culture." However, South Oregon University security guards thought it was student vandalism and disposed of it.

RIDDLE ME THIS

The **Paul Harvey Riddle** is a question which, while attributed to American radio disc jockey Paul Harvey, was not originated by the commentator. As American folklore decrees, the answer confounds scholars but 90% of children get it immediately:

"What is greater than God? More evil than the devil? The poor have it, the rich need it, and if you eat it, you'll die?" Look up the answer on the Internet.

THESE PAULS ARE CLEVERER THAN YOU...

Austrian-born philosopher **Paul Feyerabend** (1924-1994) is most famous for his rejection of the existence of methodological rules governing scientific progress. He believes that science progressing according to universal, fixed laws is inaccurate and that scientific fact triumphs due to the strength of the culture and myth that surrounds the theory. Or, dominant cultures provide scientific 'fact', not trial and error.

"Knowledge is not a series of self-consistent theories that converges toward an ideal view; it is rather an ever increasing ocean of mutually incompatible (and perhaps even incommensurable) alternatives; each single theory, each fairy tale, each myth that is part of the collection forcing the others into greater articulation and all of them contributing, via this process of competition, to the development of our consciousness." Paul Feyeraband

See? Simple.

Born in 1868, Belgian **Paul Otlet** was an absolute genius who conceived the computer and the Internet almost six decades before Tim Berners-Lee released the first web browser. In 1896, Otlet described a machine that would simultaneously access aural, literal and visual information describing it as a "radiated library and televised book".

Otlet was obsessed with the standardisation of information. His (successful) life crusade was the global adoption of the standard American 3 inch x 5 inch index cards, the ones which, until the advent of telecommunications, were used in library catalogues around the world.

"A compromise is the art of dividing a cake in such a way that everyone believes that he has got the biggest piece."
Paul Gauguin

Paul Rothemund, of the California Institute of Technology, used strands of DNA to create the world's smallest smiley face. Rothemund constructs faces that measure a thousand times smaller than the width of a human hair. Among his other accomplishments include a miniature map of the United States and South America, which is smaller than a bacterium.

"Mathematics is order and beauty at its purest, order that transcends the physical world." **Paul Hauffman** *The Man Who Loves Only Numbers, The Atlantic Magazine*, November, 1987

Type www.paul.com in your internet address field and what do you get? "We formulate strategy, optimise results, and empower entrepreneurs" (whatever that means). www.paul.com belongs to PN, who profess: "PN provides outsourced business development, marketing and project management for the computer software, internet services and telecommunications industries." It is managed by sharp cookie **Paul E. Niedermeyer**, who originally founded whois.net. Today he helps companies acquire and sell internet domain names and toll free numbers, design and execute marketing and project management campaigns, with technical requirements for internet software solutions.

Clever, probably very rich, but let's hope we never sit down next to him at dinner.

"A man who is 'of sound mind' is one who keeps the inner madman under lock and key." **Paul Valery**

Lewis Paul was the English inventor who devised the first power spinning machine, in co-operation with John Wyatt. The device had two sets of rollers which travelled at different speeds. This drew out a sliver of wool to the right thickness before spinning it. It was the forerunner to the Spinning Jenny.

Sir Paul M. Nurse won the 2001 Nobel Prize for Physiology or Medicine for discovering key regulators of the cell cycle. His research demonstrated that 'cdk1' genes served as a master switch, regulating the timing of cell-cycle events, such as division. His findings have facilitated advancements in cancer research.

"If we go back to the beginning we shall find that ignorance and fear created the gods; that fancy, enthusiasm, or deceit adorned or disfigured them; that weakness worships them; that credulity preserves them, and that custom, respect and tyranny support them in order to make the blindness of men serve their own interests." French-German author, philosopher and one of Europe's self-described atheists, **Paul-Henri Thiry, Baron d'Holbach**

Westminster Abbey's **Chapel of St. Paul** is the final resting place of the father of the modern postal system, Rowland Hill. He invented and developed the concept of a postage stamp.

Portuguese explorer **Paulo da Gama** was the older brother of Vasco da Gama. In 1497, Paul and Vasco became the first men to travel around the base of Africa's Cape of Good Hope and sail to India. Paulo's boat, the *Sao Rafael* measured 27 metres long, 8.5 metres wide, had a draft (the distance between the waterline and the bottom of the boat) of 2.3 metres, and carried around 80 men. The vessel sank on the return home leaving Paulo to join Vasco's boat, the *Sao Gabriel*. However, already sick, Paulo deteriorated and died in the Azores.

Sir Paul Edmund de Strzelecki was an imposing, if poor, Polish nobleman and explorer who was, in 1839, the first man to discover gold in Australia. In fact, The Strzelecki Desert, located in the far north of South Australia, south-west Queensland and western New South Wales, is named after him.

AND THESE ARE NOT...

Paul Cooksley was in the studio audience of *Top of the Pops* a record 43 times between 1988 and 2004.

Paul Manarang couldn't believe his luck when he won $100,000 on the California lottery. However, he wasn't so lucky when it came to collecting his loot. Manarang, inexplicably, waited 180 days to collect his winnings – it was later claimed he waited for tax reasons. On the last day he strode up to collect his bounty. Imagine his devastation when Lotto officials informed him he miscounted and had arrived on day 181!

"I never predict anything, and I never will"
Paul Gascoigne

In January 2006, **Paul James Stewart Scott**, 54, left 'Greeny', his parrot, a $500,000 fortune. Stewart, along with partner Patricia Borosik, 49, did so shortly before committing suicide.

North Dakota farmer **Paul Smokov** doesn't need high-tech equipment to forecast the weather; he consults pig spleens. After years of correct predictions, in November 2007, Smokov, 84, peered at two glistening, foot-long brown organs and told reporters: "It looks like a normal year with no major storms. That's what the spleens tell me." He was correct.

Paul Schlesselman, 18, was one of two right-wing white supremacists who were hatching a plot to kill Barack Obama shortly before the American Presidential election of November 2008. The two men did not expect to be successful. They had planned to drive as fast as they could toward Obama and shoot at him from the windows of their car while wearing white tuxedos and top hats.

AND HE MAY BE...

Paul Hughes-Barlow, known as Punditt Maharaj, has been a palmist and tarot card reader on Brighton beach for more than 20 years.

PAULY YOU CAN DRIVE MY CAR

In the history of Formula One motor racing, there
have been eight drivers named Paul. Frenchman **Paul
Belmondo** was useless but was, for a time, Princess
Stéphanie of Monaco's lover. There was Englishman **Paul
Emery**, Australian **Paul England**, who built and raced
his own car in 1957, and **Paul Frère** from Belgium, who
participated in eleven Grands Prix, achieved one podium
finish and eleven championship points. He also won the
1960 Le Mans 24-hour race. Turn 15 at the Circuit de
Spa-Francorchamps, formerly the first part of the Stavelot
corner, was renamed in his honour after he became a well-
respected post-career journalist.

America's Indy 500 was part of the Formula 1 World
Championship from 1950 to 1960. Born in 1925, American
Paul Goldsmith was a NASCAR driver who competed
in the 500 and, subsequently, in the three Indy 500/World
Championship races, earning six World Championship
points.

Australian **Paul Hawkins**, the son of a racing
motorcyclist-turned-church minister, participated in three
Grands Prix. He is one of only two drivers to have crashed
into the harbour in Monaco during the principality race.

German **Paul Pietsch**'s finest hour came in the 1939
German Grand Prix. He led from lap two until the ignition

failed, making him drop down to third. Incredibly, his car was a private entry.

American **Paul Russo** was another American to race F1 in the 1950s. Russo participated in eight World Championship races, set one fastest lead lap, finished on the podium once and accumulated a total of 8.5 World Championship points.

Would you believe it?

After several sheep and a cow died from an overdose of marijuana in southern Brazil, farm worker **Paulo Sergio Goulart** confessed to authorities that it was his fault. However, he hadn't broken any laws. Goulart had discovered plastic-wrapped blocks of cannabis hidden in a crib and fed it to the animals, assuming it was alfalfa.

In 2006, American **Paul Whisker** was driving his mother, Catherine, behind an ambulance carrying her husband, Lester, who'd had a heart attack. Incredibly, Catherine Whisker too had a heart attack. The couple were admitted to the emergency area side-by-side, where they died within five minutes of each other.

In 1993, Welsh wildlife researchers were studying the migratory habits of a micro-chipped salmon when it climbed up a riverbank and onto dry land. The salmon was found resting on the kitchen table of **Paul Williams**, along with two others. Game wardens immediately arrested him for poaching.

Paul Daulton of Surrey runs one of the world's most expensive car washes. Take your motor in and you'll be given a bill totalling £5,000! The car wash goes through over fifty different phases and takes almost a fortnight. Dalton spends over 64 hours on each car for what he calls the 'Pinnacle Wash' treatment. It includes a citrus degreaser, ph neutral shampoo, microscopic clay for mirror finish, ultra-sound, 1,000th of a millimetre buffing, lacquering re-levelling and a hand-warmed wax that sets harder than concrete.

OSCAR WINNERS NAMED PAUL

1935 Assistant Director: *The Lives of a Bengal Lancer*
Paul Wing

1936 Actor: *The Story of Louis Pasteur*
Paul Muni as Louis Pasteur

1940 Music (Original Score): *Pinocchio*
Paul J. Smith

1940 Art Direction (B&W): *Pride and Prejudice*
Paul Groesse

1943 Actor: *Watch on the Rhine*
Paul Lukas as Kurt Muller

1944 Art Direction (B&W): *Gaslight*
Paul Huldschinsky

1946 Art Direction (Colour): *The Yearling*
Paul Groesse

1948 Special Effects: *Portrait of Jennie*
Paul Eagler

1948 Film Editing: *The Naked City*
Paul Weatherwax

1949 Art Direction (Colour): *Little Women*
Paul Groesse

1951 Original Screenplay: *Seven Days to Noon*
Paul Dehn

1952 Art Direction (Colour): *Moulin Rouge*
Paul Sherriff

1953 Song: Secret Love from *Calamity Jane*
Paul Francis Webster

1953 Art Direction (Colour): *The Robe*
Paul S. Fox

1955 Music (Song): *Love Is a Many-Spendored Thing*
Paul Francis Webster

1956 Art Direction (Colour): *The King and I*
Paul S. Fox

1963 Art Direction (Colour): *Cleopatra*
Paul S. Fox

1965 Music (Song): The Shadow of Your Smile from *The Sandpiper*
Paul Francis Webster

1966 Actor: *A Man for All Seasons*
Paul Scofield as Sir Thomas More

1974 Short Film (Live Action): *One-Eyed Men Are Kings*
Paul Claudon

1976 Music (Original Score): Evergreen Love Theme from *A Star Is Born*
Paul Williams

1977 Film Editing: *Star Wars*
Paul Hirsch

1978 Art Direction: *Heaven Can Wait*
Paul Sylbert

1978 Original Song: Last Dance from *Thank God It's Friday*
Paul Jabara

1981 Short Film (Live Action): *Violet*
Paul Kemp

1984 Documentary Short: *The Stone Carvers*
Paul Wagner

1986 Actor in a leading role: *The Color of Money*
Paul Newman as Eddie Felson

1993 Jean Hersholt Humanitarian Award:
Paul Newman

1995 Make-Up: *Braveheart*
Paul Pattison

2005 Best Picture: *Crash*
Paul Haggis

2005 Original Screenplay: *Crash*
Paul Haggis

2005 Music (Original Song): It's Hard Out Here for a Pimp
from *Hustle & Flow*
Paul Beauregard

When Paul Newman was asked for his ideal epitaph, he couldn't resist having a quick jibe at anyone who ever doubted his acting credentials: "Here lies Paul Newman who died a flop because his eyes turned brown."

❧

PAUL THE SHOWMAN

The first one-man 'swim' crossing of the English Channel was completed in just less than 24 hours in 1875 by the self-titled Fearless Frogman **Captain Paul Boyton** of the USA in an inflatable rubber suit. The suit allowed the wearer to float on his back, using a double-sided paddle to propel himself, feet-forward. In 1895, he bought sixteen acres of land and opened the aquatic Sea Lion Park on Coney Island, fenced the property and charged admission. It was the first permanent amusement park in North America. It would later become Coney Island Amusement Park.

Too much time on their hands?

Paul Tavilla holds the world record for catching a grape in his mouth from the greatest height. In July 2007, Paul caught a red grape dropped from 520ft 5ins. In 1991, Paul caught a grape thrown 327ft 6ins, this time setting the record for longest grape catch on level ground.

In 1969, Australian **Paul Tully** set a record for potato chip eating by consuming thirty two-ounce bags 24.5 minutes, without a drink.

Paul Grobman's book *Vital Statistics* claims that the United States has more lawyers per capita than any other country in the world – one for every 274 people. In China, the ratio is one for every 12,745 people. Incredibly, in Washington, D.C. the figure rises to one for every 14 residents.

Paul Goldmark invented the LP (long-playing) record in 1948. Although it has had a decline in popularity, there are still 10 million LPs sold every year.

The most expensive M&M in the world sold for $1,500 in 2004. The price was due to the fact that it had been aboard **Paul Allen**'s SpaceShipOne, the privately funded human spaceflight.

Lt. Paul Robert, sheriff in Ascension, Louisiana, was the reporting officer when, in 2006, 16-year-old Jacob White apparently shot and killed himself during a game of Russian roulette. He was smoking marijuana with friends when he apparently shot himself. See, drugs can kill.

When **Pope John Paul II** visited Miami in September 1987 vendors sold T-shirts reading "I saw the Pope" in Spanish, "el Papa". However, some incorrectly translated the phrase using "la papa" which reads: "I saw the potato".

In 1996, 38-year-old **Paul Shimkonis** from Florida tried to sue a lapdancing bar after claiming he had suffered whiplash when a dancer dropped both her large breasts on top of his head. Shimkonis told the court: "It was like two cement bags hitting me. I saw stars. I've not been myself since."

There is every chance we have missed a Paul, or two.

Let us know at **www.stripepublishing.co.uk**

ACKNOWLEDGMENTS

Thanks to Dan Tester at Stripe Publishing for his help and support throughout all stages of the publication.

RECOMMENDED WEBSITES

www.laterlife.com
www.newadvent.org
www.russianbells.com
www.pbs.org
www.imdb.com
www.paulmckenna.com
www.eauk.org
www.irishcultureandcustoms.com
www.contemporarywriters.com
www.paulfarley.com
www.bookmarksmagazine.com
www.artcyclopedia.com
www.bbc.co.uk
www.urbandictionary.com
www.iep.utm.edu
www.eol.org
www.homeofheroes.com
www.dickshovel.com
www.eyewitnesstohistory.com
www.chewednews.com
www.newsoftheweird.com